# MORPHOLOGICAL CREATIVITY:

# THE MIRACLE OF YOUR HIDDEN BRAIN POWER

*Every man who knows how to read has it in his power to magnify himself, to multiply the ways in which he exists, to make his life full, significant and interesting.*

—Aldous Huxley

# MORPHOLOGICAL CREATIVITY:

# THE MIRACLE OF YOUR HIDDEN BRAIN POWER

A Practical Guide to the Utilization
of Your Creative Potential

By MYRON S. ALLEN

PRENTICE-HALL, INC., Englewood Cliffs, N.J.

LIBRARY OF CONGRESS
CATALOG CARD NUMBER: 62-14185

*First printing..........August, 1962*
*Second printing......December, 1962*

PRINTED IN THE UNITED STATES OF AMERICA

60107—B&P

Dedicated
With Grateful Appreciation
To My Wife Dorothy
And to My Sons Donald, Richard, David

# PREFACE

*Morphological creativity* is not a complicated concept, although it may be used to present complex ideas. Essentially, it is a process for creating new ideas by analyzing the form and structure of existing ones and changing the relationships of their components. The example following will show that the basic technic of morphological creativity is very simple:

### *A morphological plan for creative writing*

A problem that constantly faces any writer is to see, and to present, the relationship between the element with which he is concerned. In my own efforts to include as wide a variety of illustrative applications as possible, I made use of the morphological display that follows.

| *Areas of Living* | *Problem Systems* |
|---|---|
| A. SELF | A. FINANCE |
| B. FAMILY | B. DISCIPLINE |
| C. OCCUPATION | C. HEALTH |
| D. COMMUNITY | D. ESTEEM-POWER |
| E. COUNTRY | E. EDUCATION |
| F. WORLD | F. COMMUNICATION |
| G. CHURCH | G. RECREATION |

Each of the *areas of living* given in column 1 may be related to any of the problem systems of column 2. This will obviously suggest forty-nine types of applications for me to use. If you will visualize each column as being printed on a movable slide so that it will go up and down the page, you can easily see the forty-nine possible positions, each indicating one relationship.

The movable slides are called parameters, and they may also be arranged in concentric circles. A parameter is a constant whose value varies with the circumstances of its application.

This is a book written especially for the person who wants his life to count for as much as possible. For the person who feels that he has not achieved what he should have, and who has faith that if his inherent potentials were utilized that he would enjoy a richer, more satisfying, life.

In the book you will find many familiar ideas. The value of the book lies not in the number of new ideas presented, but in the new ideas that are developed by the synthesis of old ideas. The morphological method, by which your own ideas and those of your associates are synthesized, is a very new and extremely powerful tool for creative thinking, problem solving, and decision making. The most complex problem may be expressed in a simple, readily understood form, and when the real problem in a situation is clearly understood then efficient work on solutions is possible. Many of the blocks to the utilization of your creative potentials are pointed out and the means of converting them into positive power.

All these things can be yours if you will read creatively. This means to *receive* the ideas presented without immediate evaluation, to first try them out as directed, to look for all possible good in an idea—instead of going along with the person who is blocking himself by looking for reasons why a new idea might not be good, and so may be dropped without necessitating the adjustment that might be necessary if the idea were to be adopted.

A morphological diagram of the entire book follows. You will be helped in your reading if you refer to it from time to time, as the true significance of any one idea lies in its relationships to the other ideas of the book.

MYRON S. ALLEN

| Introduction WHAT MORPHOLOGICAL CREATIVITY CAN DO FOR YOU | Chapter 1. HOW TO HAVE A LIFE WORTH WHILE | Chapter 2. HOW TO GET A MILLION IDEAS | Chapter 3. HOW TO CONTROL IDEAS | Chapter 4. HOW TO THINK CREATIVELY | Chapter 5. HOW TO BE CREATIVE |
|---|---|---|---|---|---|
| | | | | | |
| 1 How to be Happy | 1 A Life that Satisfies | 1 Avoid Scarcity of Ideas in the Midst of Plenty | 1 Be the Master, Not the Slave, of Your Ideas | 1 Free the Frozen Assets of Your Mind | 1 Develop Initiative |
| 2 Life Purpose and Creative Power | 2 Freedom in an Age of Conformity | 2 Use All of Your Sources of Ideas | 2 Invest Your Ideas at Compound Interest | 2 Be Original | 2 Develop Total Sensitivity |
| 3 Freedom is Still Your Right and Privilege | 3 Self-Confidence Comes from Believing in Yourself | 3 Help-Don't Hinder-Idea Production | 3 Synthesize All Available Ideas Before Evaluating Any | 3 Avoid Bit Thinking | 3 Develop Total Flexibility |
| 4 The Nature of Morphological Creativity | 4 Conservation of Creative Energy | 4 Don't be a Slave to Habits and Customs | 4 Determine the Total Meaning of Synthesized Ideas | 4 Use Your Imagination | 4 Develop Verbal Fluency |
| 5 Your Creative Power | 5 An Objective Precedes Creativity | 5 Use Ideas on Hand to Suggest Others Without Limit | 5 Avoid Prejudice By Synthesizing Ideas Before Analyzing Problems | 5 Utilize the Unlimited Subconscious Power | 5 Respect Your Need to be Creative |
| 6 Foundations of Morphological Creativity | 6 Problem Solving is Applied Creativity | 6 Utilize to the Maximum Your Unlimited Imagination | 6 Be Sure that the King Value is the Center of All Evaluations Made | 6 Be Open-Minded | 6 Invent Systematically |
| 7 Creativity in Today's World | 7 Creativity in the Home | 7 Utilize the Broad Principles of Ideation | 7 Develop Internal Standards of Evaluation | 7 Reduce Mental Tensions | 7 Become a Genius |
| | | | | | |

| Chapter 6. HOW TO GET ALONG WITH ANYBODY | Chapter 7. HOW TO HELP OTHERS TO BE CREATIVE | Chapter 8. HOW TO MAKE GOOD DECISIONS | Chapter 9. HOW TO SOLVE PROBLEMS | Chapter 10. HOW TO BE A CREATIVE SUPERVISOR |
|---|---|---|---|---|
| | | | | |
| 1 Develop Four-Way Communication | 1 Get Everybody Into the Act | 1 Determine the Basic Pattern of a Situation | 1 Develop Problem Sensitivity | 1 Establish a Creative Atmosphere |
| 2 Work Understandingly | 2 Utilize Differences of Opinion | 2 Utilize Multiple Viewpoints | 2 Approach Problems With Confidence | 2 Develop Sensitivity to Change |
| 3 Consider the Same Problem | 3 Substitute Cooperation for Misguided Competition | 3 Consider All of the Essential Elements | 3 Determine the Real Problem to be Solved | 3 Conduct Harmonious and Constructive Conferences |
| 4 Be Sensitive to Feedback | 4 Provide Anonymity to Members of Non-Homogeneous Groups | 4 Respect and Utilize Your Intuitive Powers | 4 Produce Multiple Solutions | 4 Avoid the Effects of Isolated Specialization |
| 5 Respect the Fundamental Dignity of People | 5 Lessen Resistance to New Ideas | 5 Be Sure that the Proposals being Considered Refer to Same Problem | 5 Utilize Progressive Intuition | 5 Enable the Plodder and the Soarer to Work together |
| 6 Be Concerned For the General Welfare | 6 Respect the Need For Every Person to Achieve His Potential | 6 Reduce Mental Stress in Minds of Those Affected by Your Decisions | 6 Display the Total Solution for the Real Problem | 6 Do Things the Easy Way |
| 7 Strive to Increase Good Will | 7 Use Environmental Stimulators of Creativity | 7 Reduce False Values | 7 Be Familiar With the Basic Steps of Morphological Problem Solving | 7 Do Things the Simple Way. |
| | | | | |

# CONTENTS

# MORPHOLOGICAL CREATIVITY:

# THE MIRACLE OF YOUR HIDDEN BRAIN POWER

## Introduction

---

# WHAT MORPHOLOGICAL CREATIVITY CAN DO FOR YOU

The purpose of this book is to help *you* to achieve the life you seek—and *only* you can find this life for yourself. You will find this to be a simple, down-to-earth book, written to be understood and full of things that you can use immediately to enrich every part of your life.

### 1. How to Be Happy

Are you looking for ways to a happier and a more useful life? You can have this life worth while by developing your own potentials, thus becoming:

- More efficient
- Free from internal and external barriers to creative achievement
- Free from prejudice in your thinking
- Able to suggest many solutions to any problem
- Independent and versatile in your thinking
- Able to produce ideas in unlimited quantities
- Able to invent new products systematically
- Sure of making good decisions
- Able to get along with people, even under pressure
- Free from unresolved frustration and tension
- Able to make full use of your intuitive powers

***The secret of happiness is to feel useful***

Your maximum usefulness—in your home, at your work, and everywhere else depends upon the utilization of your creative power. You will find in the book many suggestions and methods that have helped others to be more creative, and which will also help you. The ideas presented have been gathered in personal interviews with truly creative people who have done all kinds of wonderful things. They have been thoroughly tested in courses in *Applied Creativity* taught in the Industrial Inservice Division of the University of Southern California, in Management Consulting situations, in a Family Relations Institution, in Personal Counseling, and in College Physics Classes. You may use what you read with complete confidence.

***The power of a purpose***

One objective of this book, perhaps its greatest one, is to help you, the reader, to find your purpose in life. For as you find this purpose you will be able to make use of your own creative power —and those of your associates—that both you and your country may not only survive the present world power struggle but rise to ever-increasing, true achievements.

## 2. Life Purpose and Creative Power

***The secret of creative power***

About five years ago I set out to discover what highly creative persons had, that the rest of us ordinary persons did not have. I held long interviews with hundreds of this country's most outstanding creative persons, in science, business, art, music, and other fields. I was surprised and delighted to find nothing at all in the endowment of even the most highly creative person that has been withheld from any one of us. Instead, I discovered that these so-called geniuses were able to express their creative power because of something that they *did not* have. I found great creative achievers to be more free of the self-imposed blocks that inhibit the creativity of most people. At various places in this book these blocks will be discussed and ways of eliminating them suggested.

### *You can depend upon your creative power*

Are you often afraid to express yourself? Why?

Timidity usually stems from genuine doubts of one's ability to be creative. The average person does not trust *himself* to be creative enough to produce needed ideas. As you apply the principles given in this book, your appreciation of—and faith in—your own creative power will become stronger and stronger.

You will also find that the expression of creativity in one area of your life will release additional creative power, so that you will be able to find a good solution to a problem that has been blocking your progress in some other area.

### *Creativity and courage*

As you become conscious of your truly tremendous latent creative power you will lose many of the fears that are now preventing the achievements that you seek. You will find that even the fear of the unknown will lessen, and that you will once again seek for adventure wherever it is to be found.

Every person actually has available to him a tremendous amount of knowledge which, if handled with confidence and competence, will enable him to solve a great many more problems than he may feel qualified to touch.

Courage and creativity are always found together. The genius is one who has developed confidence in his ability to succeed—and who is willing to try, even when the successful achievement of his objective may be greatly delayed.

## 3. Freedom is Still Your Right and Privilege

### *Individual freedom in group activity*

Through creative association you will develop your ability to achieve freedom while conforming to group patterns. You will be able to defend yourself against pressures, and find plenty of time to do the things that you really want to do. Your ability to participate in, and to direct, group activities will be increased. You will better understand the effects on your own creative achievements, of the attitudes that you hold toward your associates.

### *Creativity and society*

All things remain yet to be done, or to be done over. You live one *total* life, and not several *separate* lives. The principles and methods presented in this book are directly applicable to all areas of living.

The increasing complexities of our society demand the maintenance of certain interdependencies. It is a challenging task to live in such a way that you may realize your own potentialities with the minimum of social interference.

## 4. The Nature of Morphological Creativity

### *Morphological creativity is a blue-print for creative thinking*

Just as a well drawn blue-print enables a qualified technician to utilize the results of extensive research, so does *morphological creativity* make possible the utilization of your potentials. This book provides a step-by-step plan by means of which you will be able to perform *systematically* much of the sort of creative thinking that great geniuses have always done *intuitively*.

It might be of interest if you looked at the morphological charts of some complex concepts, although not to attempt to interpret them at this time The diagrams for *Creativity,* for *Morphology,* and for Jet Engines, to be found in the appendix, are suggested as interesting applications of morphological principles.

### *A morphological design for a book*

This book was planned, organized, and written in accordance with morphological principles. It is, so far as I know, the first one so designed to be published in this country. *Morphological Astronomy,* by Dr. F. Zwicky, of the California Institute of Technology, was published in Germany and at this time is the only other morphological book available in this country.

Perhaps you might like to look at the morphological chart of this book, immediately following the preface. On this one chart are shown the main objective of the book, the sub-objectives, the basic problems needing to be solved and their basic solutions. This chart indicates a step-by-step process by means of which you can increase your own creativity.

## 5. Your Creative Power

***Your creative power is unlimited***

The secret of creative power is knowledge that its supply is inexhaustible within every individual—and then the willingness to act in accordance with this belief.

***Use your hidden creative power***

It is well known that most of what we have learned remains well below the conscious level. We all have had experiences when this hidden treasure is retrieved following the application of suitable stimuli. We have awakened in the morning with solutions to a problem that were beyond our reach while working on the problem the previous evening. In the following chapter a method of *producing* intuition, through improving the efficiency of the subconscious mind, will be introduced.

***Your success in life depends upon your being creative***

As you already have what it takes to succeed, you now need only to utilize these creative potentials. Get out of your own way. Release your almost untapped creative resources and then no person or condition can block you.

***Reduce mental strain***

While a moderate amount of pressure helps to awaken one's lazy initiative, an excess of stress that cannot be absorbed into action will set up mental stresses that block or greatly inhibit creative achievement. *Morphological Creativity* offers you principles and technics by means of which you will be able to reduce your own mental strain by doing what every creative genius does, utilizing the unlimited resources of the subconscious.

## 6. Foundations of Morphological Creativity

### *Acknowledgments*

The writer is deeply grateful to those whose assistance and encouragement have made this book a reality. The number of these persons is far too large to make individual mention feasible. But to three men, in particular, I am so greatly indebted that I would be intellectually dishonest were I not to make special acknowledgment.

Dr. J. P. Guilford, Director of the Aptitudes Project in the Department of Psychology at the University of Southern California, through a special staff appointment, made available to me all of his monumental work in the psychology of creativity. In his outstanding and unique book, *Personality,* Dr. Guilford presents the results of his original investigations into the factors of personality, including those upon which creativity is based. The book is one of the McGraw-Hill series in Psychology, 1959.

Dr. Alex F. Osborn, co-founder of Batten, Barton, Durstine and Osborn, and chairman of the Board of the Creative Education Foundation, by my appointment as member of the Advisory Council of the Foundation and as a leader of the Creative Problem Institute, made available to me the vast resources of those organizations. In *Applied Imagination* Dr. Osborn has freely shared the great principles of creative thinking and creative problem solving that have made his business career such a tremendous success. Dr. Osborn treats Creativity and Creative Problem Solving in a far broader sense than the relatively limited aspect of the simple technic for idea finding known as Brainstorming. Charles Scribner's Sons, Revised 1960.

Dr. F. Zwicky, professor of Astrophysics at the California Institute of Technology, introduced me to *morphology*—a philosophy and a plan of thinking—that has made possible the synthesis of the heretofore unorganized concepts of creativity. His book,

*Morphological Astronomy*, obtainable from the College Bookstore at the California Institute of Technology in Pasadena, explains how the principles of morphology made possible many significant discoveries in astronomy.

## 7. Creativity in Today's World

### *One world—one problem*

The whole world is becoming more and more closely interconnected. Old provincial philosophies are being made obsolete. There seems to be little creative effort in the formation of our international policies. Our problems in world crisis, as at other times, can only be solved creatively. Ideas such as communism will have to be fought with newer and better ideas if the battle is to be won.

### *Mass opinion and educated opinion*

To be happy one must make positive contributions to society. Accordingly, your happiness to a great extent depends on whether or not you express yourself creatively. We have evolved a society in which mass opinion, rather than the best educated opinion, is in control. Democracy has been evolving into something very different from that with which we started.

### *Is satisfaction possible in routine work?*

It is increasingly difficult to find satisfaction, as a producer, in routine work. This lack is of especial significance when years on a job, rather than outstanding performance, brings promotion. A higher level of creativity is the only possible answer. Management calls loudly for creativity on the part of employees, which they usually are not permitted to express. The closeness of a person working on a routine job to the problems innate in that job gives him a fine opportunity to see his job creatively. It is this knowledge and creative potential that is being so much wasted in the industrial world today.

# 1

## HOW TO HAVE A LIFE WORTHWHILE

One of the best known systems engineers of the International Business Machines Corporation, when I was asking him about his phenomenal success in solving difficult problems, expressed his philosophy in this way:

*"If it* OUGHT *to be done, It* CAN *be done,*<br>IF *it can be done,* I *can do it."*

The turning point in the lives of outstanding American scientists came when they realized that they had the ability to solve problems *by themselves,* that they could take on important responsibilities and handle them successfully. But most important of all was the realization that they themselves were important sources of information, and capable of doing original work.

### 1. A Life that Satisfies

***Five steps to worthwhile living***

If you were to be given one wish, with the promise that it would be granted, what would you wish for? Health, wealth, cars, a new home, travel? Or would you ask for that which you hoped these gifts would bring you—A Life that Satisfies?

What is it that makes life worth living—in your home, in your job, in your church, at your club, in your community, and in your country? It is the achievement of maximum usefulness, as you seek to find out and to fulfill your own life purpose.

In worthwhile living there is a cyclic sequence of events that occurs over and over again wherever successful living is to be found, these are:

a. Becoming sensitive to a life purpose
b. Establishing basic objectives
c. Determining the problems needing to be solved
d. Finding solutions to the problems
e. Evaluating results of applying the solutions

### *Creativity is infinite in scope*

Creativity finds expression, or can, over the entire range of your life. There is no more an end to creativity than there is to the universe, or to time itself. Creativity is more than a process, and a product—it is a way of life. As Benjamin Franklin said, "To cease to think creatively is to cease to live."

### *The universal purpose of life*

The great objective of life is *purposeful growth*—through the creative expression of potential power. With this concept as the heart of a life philosophy, decisions will be made and solutions of problems proposed, in terms of their effects on the growth of all persons involved.

## 2. Freedom in an Age of Conformity

### *Has modern man lost his independence?*

The newer interdependent economic system is very threatening to many people, particularly those who got along satisfactorily under the former system. In the time of one generation ago you would be learning simultaneously the art of *living* and the art of *making* a living. Now, the average man sees himself as a group-dependent man, not as self-sufficient. He finds himself in desperate need of access to new frontiers, *within* the framework of an interdependent economic system. Then, too, the average man is no longer a self-contained unit. His two major roles of producer and consumer are almost separate from one another.

### *Early settlers were self-sufficient*

During the settlement of our country, each settler was relatively self-sufficient. There was an open land frontier, with culturally ideal conditions for promoting individual creativity. We cannot go back to the actual frontier conditions because we are now so heavily dependent on one another. We now have to move *together,* finding new ways to help each other to achieve individual and group fulfillment.

### *Better human relations*

The most pressing need of our times is for the development of better human relations. By becoming more creative, and by helping others to become more creative, we can live lives that are marked by better understanding of one another.

### *Doing what you want to do is not selfish*

If what you want to do is more worth while to yourself than something that somebody else wants you to do, then please yourself. Why should you allow somebody else to run your life?

Of course, there are many things both on and off the job that you do because it is wise or right for you to do them. But you should keep these entirely separate from the great host of activities you could engage in just because someone else thinks that you should be doing them. Just be honest. If someone calls up and asks if you are doing anything this evening, tell him that you are. Especially if, from your knowledge of the person calling, you can easily find something else to do that is more worthwhile or more enjoyable for you than what he will probably propose. If you want to go up on the hill with your wife to watch the lights of the city below, tell the would-be visitor that you are just on your way out, but will try to make a date sometime next week.

### *Time to do what you want*

What would you do if you did have enough time to do what you want? You *do* have time, so why not use it, and find out how much fun it is to do what you really want to do. It is a very simple matter—just decide for yourself the relative importance of the many things open for you to do, and always work down from the *top* of the list.

### *Individual freedom within practical conformity*

No human being can be truly happy unless he is expressing creatively his inherent potentials. Yet, within a culture of rapidly increasing complexity and change, there is an ever-growing pressure to conform.

How may a person be free and restricted at the same time? Are we stuck tightly in an impossible situation, where the creative individual is to be looked upon as a potential trouble-maker? Is it any longer possible to gain relief from the yoke of custom and convention?

There are, it is true, a great many instances where individuality brings catastrophe. You simply cannot drive, with safety to yourself or other drivers, in the wrong direction on a one-way street. Neither can you develop your own personal alphabet, if you desire to communicate with your neighbors.

Demonstrated excellence, alone, is no guarantee of freedom. We may be prevented from performing some task, from teaching a course, or from expressing an opinion, simply because of the fear, the inertia, or the plain "cussedness" of some other individual or group.

### *Reaction to conformity pressure*

The natural reaction to the blocking of creative thinking is to fight back. Again, even though progress is being made in the acceptance of an idea, the relative slowness is quite frustrating.

How, then, are you to satisfy, at the same time, both the external reactionary forces under which most of us have to work and the compelling urge within for creative expression?

This is a crucial question that should be answered now, because we can expect *more* regulation, in some areas of our lives, rather than less. Yet we *must not* surrender to reactionary conformity if we are to survive as a nation.

### *How to have freedom while conforming*

Yes, there *is* a positive solution to the problem of freedom with conformity. The solution is independent of all environmental conditions, and is independent of everybody—with the one exception of the would-be creative person himself.

There are more areas of life in which one may act as creatively as he wishes than areas in which he must conform. As you move freely in these unrestricted areas, the frustration that you would have felt had you moved and fought only in the restricted areas does not trouble you.

The writer has been for many years an instructor in physics in a very conservative institution that wishes its staff to teach traditional material in a traditional manner. In years gone by, our efforts to force the tempo of creative advance was most painful to all concerned. Now, instead of exerting high pressure to introduce the principles of creative thinking and problem solving—which are not officially desired—we have freely expressed our creative desires in tuition classes for engineering, research, and management personnel. These classes have been conducted exactly as I have deemed to be best for their members. I have advanced much further myself by devoting all of my creative energy in places where creativity was desired. I have had rich opportunities to apply my creative principles to the problems of today's world, and even to some of tomorrow, instead of being limited to treating dead problems in an archaic manner.

While I deeply regret that my students of physics are not receiving the training in creative thinking that they need, and have the right to receive if they are to meet effectively on-coming responsibilities, I am not personally frustrated. I have, in other areas, been able to gain the increased self-confidence that comes only through success.

Conformity and individuality are not mutually exclusive. They can, and they will, continue to exist side by side in the years that lie ahead. Individuality brings progress. Conformity enables *groups* to exist, and to protect themselves from too rapid or too revolutionary changes.

### 3. Self-Confidence Comes from Believing in Yourself

***Realizing your potentials***

Your talents are constantly craving outlet. When this expression is blocked your frustration is really painful. The comfortable ruts that are so easy to fall into can be surmounted only by consistent creativity. It is very necessary for your psychological health that you have available the means of expressing your creative potentials.

***The fear of failure***

Terrifyingly apparent in the great majority of our population is the fear of failure. The director of one of our foremost electronic laboratories told me that he has placed his entire staff in one or the other of three categories: (1) those who are highly courageous, willing to attempt any problem that comes along; (2) those having less self-confidence and who try to avoid fundamentally new problems; (3) those with still less self-confidence who are disturbed unless they are working under quite specific direction. These same three groups are roughly *research, development,* and *production.* Converting "failure" into constructive achievement will occupy much of our attention in the pages to follow.

***Think like a creative person and you will be one***

To understand the secret of creative power you must think and act like a creative person. Some of the attributes that you will demonstrate as a creative person are: a strong interest in things and in people, an insatiable curiosity and the initiative to satisfy your curiosity, a sensitivity to problems and the needs of people, fluency, flexibility, originality, imagination and open-mindedness. The meanings of these attributes, and how they may be developed, will be encountered many times as you work through this book.

### *Self-confidence brings success*

The chairman of the board, and the builder of a great industrial empire, when I asked him about the bringing up of his phenomenally successful son said, "I frequently told him that he could do anything that he set his mind to."

### *Success develops self-confidence*

The highly important attribute of self-confidence can be developed only through successful experiences. In some mysterious way, a confident, hopeful, positive attitude produces an actual increase in available creative power. You are then able to gain an objective or solve a problem which would be beyond your ability if it were to be approached without such a confident attitude.

### *Confidence through use of your potentials*

As you learn to utilize, to a fuller extent, your own potentials and those of your associates, you will acquire a new confidence in yourself and in your ability to handle difficult problems. You will make decisions with a greater certainty, as well as more quickly.

The creative person is self-confident in those areas in which he is creative. Confidence and creativity are *always* found together. The development of one of these attributes will result in the increased expression of the other attributes.

### *Creativity in leadership*

Leaders are likely to be men who have recognized the role of creativity in their work. Otherwise they could not generate the behavior that makes them leaders. Creativity, then, may well be regarded as the heart of leadership.

Creativity in human leaderships, a large part of leadership, requires that you not only put yourself in another person's shoes, but for a time *become* that person. Seeing things as they look to *him.* Naval aviation flight surgeons discovered that, in order to render the services needed by aviation personnel, the doctors themselves had to go through the entire flight training program.

## 4. Conservation of Creative Energy

***How to increase your energy***

The demands upon our energy are increasing constantly. It seems likely that we shall be unable to increase appreciably our actual supply of physical or mental energy so it is necessary to look for ways to make better use of the energy that we do have.

You can increase the effects of your energy by concentrating on one thing at a time. It requires much less expenditure of energy to cut down a tree with a sharp axe than with a dull one. A dull axe is one with a broad edge—that requires the use of much greater force to produce cutting pressure than does a sharp axe.

If you try to do several things at once you will be less effective with any one. When many problems are confronting you, simultaneously, you will be able to concentrate your energy on one at a time by following the simple expedient of writing down each of the problems on a separate card. Arrange the problems in order of decreasing immediate importance and work on the top two or three until they have been solved, then take the next one, and so on.

***Keep prodding your initiative***

Another way that you can save a tremendous amount of time is to *begin without delay* some task—perhaps difficult or unpleasant—that you know full well you are going to have to do sooner or later. Even if the job looks impossible or endless, *start.*

Another way to get jobs done is to write them down, and place the list where you will see it frequently. I remember several such lists that my nearly ninety year old father-in-law had swinging on a board near the back door of his ranch home. Nobody expected that he would ever get all his projects completed, but he always did.

As you consider the jobs on your list you will eventually start thinking of possible methods of getting the job done. Finally you will begin on one of these jobs. You will then notice things around you, which have escaped your attention before, that will help you to get the job done. Thoughts are powerful things. No one knows just how they operate, either inside or outside the thinker. How far thoughts travel, or the extent to which they influence other people who are in a position to help complete the job you are thinking of—are unanswered but pertinent questions.

### *Plug up your energy leaks*

In addition to having more time for good living by being selective in the things you do, you should conserve your not-unlimited energy. If you yield to some secondary demand, you are very apt to make an effort to crowd in the thing that you really want to do, at the expense of food or sleep.

Anxiety, worry, and fear are a closely related trio that drain off much energy, that otherwise could be used in some form of creative expression. Anxiety is an undifferentiated reaction to a vague situation, something like trying to run away from an invisible cloud of poison gas. Worry is a repetitive action that repeats itself over and over again, instead of solving a problem —similar to a record with a scratch. Fear is a specific reaction to a known danger. Because fear is often focused, satisfying results often occur under the stimulus of fright. Many instances are on record where fear has supplied sufficient energy to enable a person to do what would ordinarily be impossible, such as lifting an overturned car in order to release a victim pinned beneath it.

In my early college teaching days, before I had learned not to waste my strength pushing against prejudiced opposition, I had little extra energy. In fact, I often had difficulty in finishing the day's work. The frustration of these years drained my energy as a short circuit drains the storage battery of a car. If you will *refuse* to be frustrated, you will have so much more energy to use that your accomplishments will make far less likely the possibility of frustration or failure.

Try acting, and thinking, as though you believed that you will get back the same kind of thoughts that you send out—and in greater quantity. You will soon find out for yourself that this is indeed a powerful truth. Your available energy will go up or down, according to the nature of thoughts that you send and receive.

### *Even a mule knows enough to rest once in a while*

You would not attempt to lift a five-hundred pound weight barehanded, unless you were a conditioned weight lifter. You would soon be so exhausted that you would have great difficulty in picking up a rock that weighed but one hundred pounds.

Many persons have mental collapses, coronary attacks, and emotional disturbances, because of too prolonged efforts on a task that is not moving toward completion.

There is an old belief that there is something meritorious in never giving up—once you have begun to solve a problem in a certain way. Ross Aiken, a famous inventor in electronics, has a favorite expression, "There *must* be another way." To his staff he says, "Don't waste too much time on a method that doesn't produce results. It usually costs less to try another way that might work better, than to keep forcing your way along a difficult path, even though it might eventually work."

President Coolidge was once asked just how it was that he had managed to escape so many of the troubles that beset earlier Presidents. Mr. Coolidge's typical New England reply was, "If I see any trouble coming toward me, I just sit still for a while. Nine times out of ten somebody else will run out and stop it before it gets to me."

This was not a lazy man's view, but that of a wise man who wanted his energy to be expended on those duties that he alone could do best.

### *Don't sell other people short—Use their brains*

Still another way of conserving your energy is to utilize the experience—and the willingness—of those about you. Six men can lift heavy beams all day without tiring. While two men could carry the same load, during an entire day three sets of two men would accomplish far less than six men working together—because the smaller groups would need to rest so often.

Over a given period, and in the right environment, six men working in a research team can achieve results that the same six men working alone could not. More and more of the problems to be solved are so complex that no single man working by himself could possibly succeed.

I once worked in a New England grinding wheel factory where the vice president opened all incoming mail. After reading the letters he handed them out to various people to handle. While the vice president was doing this clerical work, the labor cost of making the wheels had climbed to almost double the amount for which the wheels could be sold at a profit.

### *Don't work on the same problem too long at a time*

Changing your work at intervals will conserve your energy, actually requiring less to complete a given job. Most researchers like to have at least two or three projects under way at one time. When their progress on one problem becomes too little, they will switch to another job which has been "cooking" for a period of time. Scientists have told me that they almost invariably will find that they are now able to move much faster on the former problem. There are two good reasons for this accelerated progress. First, a different set of mental tools is called into action, and second, the processes of intuition have been at work while the problem was resting.

## 5. An Objective Precedes Creativity

### *The role of objectives in worthwhile living*

Is your home a well-coordinated, harmonious, relaxed, happy place—where everybody pulls together with mutual understanding? Does your home have a common objective that is accepted by all members, as a guide for individual and for group actions? It takes a "yes" answer for the second question to make possible a "yes" answer for the first question.

At your place of business is there a common objective for top management, middle management, supervision, salaried and hourly workers? Does this objective serve as a clear-cut guide for the policies of the company? Is there complete understanding and free communication throughout the entire company and with its outside public? Again, a common "yes" answer is needed.

### *What is the difference between an objective and a problem?*

An *objective* makes clear *where* you want to go. *Problems* are those barriers that must be *removed* if you are going to attain your objective. If the objective of a young man is to become a great physician, then how to procure the finances to defray the costs of his education is one of the problems.

An objective is never actually attained, but rather is approached. When a problem is solved a *goal* is reached, which—if wisely selected—marks progress toward the objective. Goals, on the way toward the physician objective, would be the completion of medical school and the acquisition of the M.D. degree.

### *A clear objective reduces argument and tension*

Most arguments arise because the persons involved are talking about *different* things. This means that the participants are trying to move toward different objectives. The next time you are present at an argument, whether a participant or not, step back a little and take a look at what each person is saying. You will usually find that there is a different objective directing the thoughts of each speaker.

If an objective is accepted that is broad enough to include the basic needs of all parties concerned, even the problems that stand in the way of achieving the objectives are usually agreed upon with little difficulty. The real problem begins when solutions are proposed.

### *Objectives must not be too limited*

While it is true that an objective that is too broad dulls the sharpness of group effort, an objective that is too narrow becomes isolated from other objectives which are together related parts of a more comprehensive objective. The detailed procedures of formulating objectives will be discussed later in several sections of the book. At this point, we are simply pointing out *why* the setting up of objectives acceptable to a group is so vital to both group and individual growth.

***Working objectives must be specific***

The basic objective, *to achieve a life worth living,* is much too broad for a direct approach. A group of people working on such an objective would be thinking of so many different problems as to apply relatively little effort to any one problem area. Sub-objectives, of a reasonable scope, greatly facilitate the identification of problems and the finding of solutions.

***Put first things first, in problem solving***

If you were building a house, you would not attempt to nail shingles on the roof before the basic roof structure had been built. Yet, more frequently than not, people attempt to offer solutions before the problem has been clearly defined—even before the objective has been established. This reversal of procedure is the cause of much fruitless argument and wasted effort.

***Resources for happiness***

High up on the list of personal attributes that make for happiness is the ability to *think* one's way out of a difficulty. Creativity is the basis of problem solving. Creativity is needed when you cannot solve a problem on the basis of experience alone.

## 6. Problem Solving is Applied Creativity

***Creativity in problem solving***

The essence of creative problem solving lies in the ability to recognize the disturbing elements of a confused situation. The number of problems that may be found in any given situation is actually unlimited, especially when the many relationships are seen that exist between the visible problems.

***How to find the real problem***

What is the *real* problem you are trying to solve? This is a question that should be asked early and often in problem solving.

No matter how good may be the solutions that you find for a problem, they will be of no value in the attainment of your objective if you are trying to solve the *wrong* problem. You have found the basic problem, the real problem, in any problem situation, when the continued asking of the question *why* brings answers that are fundamental to the achievement of your basic objective.

### *The difference between a problem and a question*

There is but *one* right answer to any *question*—such as, how much does a piece of beef weigh? However, there are *unlimited solutions* to the *problem* of cooking and serving the meat. There is *no* right or wrong solution to the problem of cooking the meat. The order of preference of the solutions depends on a great many factors, ranging from the quality and the cut of the meat to the preference of the intended diners. It is these external factors that determine the rank order of the solutions of any problem. They are sometimes called the "specifications" of the problem.

### *Offer a solution—Get an argument*

Objectives and problems are *facts* that can be agreed upon when mutually understood. Solutions are *opinions* that will always differ, until a compromise has been effected.

As mentioned earlier, there is seldom any objection raised to any worthwhile, mutually beneficial objective. The problems raised by different people—while seen as having various degrees of importance—are generally accepted as problems with little argument. Problems and objectives may be accepted because there is no specific action inherent in them. But any solution proposed will effect everybody in any way concerned with the problem. The presentation of a proposed solution to a problem is the signal for the raising of objections. If the proposed solution, no matter how good it may be, will be likely to cause changes, then it will be automatically attacked. Often the very best solutions, the novel ones, are killed before they have been seriously considered. It is often very difficult for the proponent of a novel solution to make a good showing in the argument concerning it. After being made to look bad with respect to a novel solution, the tendency is strengthened to present more standard, and less original, solutions.

### *Solving simple, obvious problems*

When a problem to be solved is limited in scope, the solutions are usually single ideas. Some of the better known plans of ideation suitable for problems of limited scope, which may be parts of complex problems, are: *Brainstorming, Attribute-Listing, Checklists* and variations of the familiar *"Buzz Session"* such as Phillips "66." These have all been described so many times in various publications that there is no point in repeating here.

### *Solving complex problems*

There is no *simple* solution to a *complex* problem. There must be a total solution if the total problem is to be solved. Smog, for example, is a very complex problem which the simple elimination of home trash burners could not possibly solve.

No source of ideas, or method of procuring them, should be overlooked in the unprejudiced search for solutions. In the chapters to follow the unique approach of *morphological creativity* to individual and group ideation will be described and illustrated. By using the morphological method you will be able to handle any number of ideas—the more the better—without confusion, and with no feeling of being overwhelmed by the sheer mass of ideas available.

A rule to remember is, that as a problem always involves more than one person, the solutions to a problem should utilize the ideas of many people. Because different people respond best to different kinds of stimuli, many ways of gathering ideas for solutions may be appropriate.

The manner in which a leader and his problem-solving group get along together, as well as their mutual acceptance of the common objective, has a great effect on the type and the quality of the solutions offered.

### *Guiding principles for solution finding*

Any solution to a problem is *one* method of removing that problem as an obstacle to progress toward an objective.

In searching for solutions, each person who is in any way associated with the problem of interest is a potential source of ideas, which may be synthesized into the solutions sought. The more people who have contributed to the solutions of a problem, the fewer persons there will be who feel compelled to oppose the solution adopted.

Problems themselves often suggest possible solutions. For example, if profits are too low on a competitive item for which the price cannot be raised, the solutions suggested are obviously to cut the costs of production and sales, or to add something to the product which will increase the sales to a point that the unit cost may be lowered.

## 7. Creativity in the Home

### *There is no place like home*

A life that satisfies is quite impossible without a satisfying home life. Here are endless opportunities for creative work in solving the many complex and pressing problems that make home interesting and active. To get the most out of children we must meet them at least fifty-one per cent of the way. Most parents are guilty of a lack of encouragement of their children's creative activity, if not actually guilty of active discouragement. Discipline, too, provides many opportunities for constructive creativity.

### *One sure way to a happy home*

A happier home is not a problem—but an objective. What are the problems in the way of attaining that objective? To find out just what problems are interfering with the achievement of a happy home, a sensitivity and an artistry are required that are frequently not utilized. When a father lines up his wife and children on the davenport, stands up before them and barks, "We must have a happier home; what are you going to do about it?" —very little will be accomplished.

Should one of the children give the often truthful answer, "Dad, you are too bossy," the father would probably begin to defend his rule as being a little firm, perhaps, but certainly just and fair. The family, after seeing that this kind of comment isn't going to get them anywhere, drops the real problem and feeds father what they think he wants to hear. Succeeding talk would tend to revolve about such matters as who should bring the trash can in from the street, allowances, and the use of the family car.

### *A new approach to family problems*

Let us look at another family scene. A trusted friend of the family has dropped in for the evening and the entire family is sitting informally around the living room. The guest finally says, "Your dad and I were talking about our families the other day. We agreed that we should be much happier as families than we are. We also agreed that it is very difficult to find out just what our families really think about things.

"Tonight, I am here as a neutral guide," the family guest continues; "tomorrow your dad will be over at my house. Both of us will gather confidential information about problems standing in the way of family happiness. A week or two later each family will hold a similar meeting, this time searching for the best solutions to the problems that have been raised. If each of you will be completely honest, and honestly complete, we shall be able to make great progress toward our objectives of happier homes."

### *Love your enemies, your friends, and yourself*

We have mentioned many ways to conserve or to acquire energy, in this chapter. But one method, so far not discussed, is the simplest, the most effective, and the least considered of all—the improvement of our own attitudes.

The holding of resentment toward anybody or anything is as wasteful of creative energy as the leaving on of your car lights or radio. Resentment is like a poisonous smog pouring out of a person. It dissipates a large share of creative energy that otherwise would be available for constructive activities. In some manner resentment inhibits the release of creative power. Don't waste time trying to understand how this occurs. Just try it out for yourself, and be convinced.

I once asked my students in a class in applied creativity, as an assignment, to find something worthy of sincere commendation in the work of an associate with whom they had the poorest relationship.

The director of training for a large West Coast industry selected a senior of his in the category designated. The director said to this man, "This is a fine piece of work that you have done. It must have taken a great deal of time and effort." The response was truly astonishing. Communication that had been blocked for years opened up. My student had radiated kindness toward his senior, who had picked it up, had amplified what he had received, and then had returned it. Some human relations problems of fifteen years standing were removed as the direct result of the student's enlightened attitude.

# 2

## HOW TO GET A MILLION IDEAS

According to the great Oxford dictionary, an idea is "the plan, or design, according to which something is created or con-constructed."

There are both large ideas and small ideas to be considered. An architect may suggest the general idea for a great resort hotel. Within this total idea are lesser ideas regarding the style and colors of carpets and drapes. These greater and lesser ideas are all related, and in a measure limit each other.

The initial concept will usually be very vague. For example, a hotel man while on a fishing trip sees a beautiful lake that is fed by many streams full of rainbow trout. He immediately visualizes a hotel full of people paying him up to $100 per day for their accommodations and recreations.

Before the architect can do more than make some general sketches, showing how a hotel could be built and not destroy the natural beauty of the spot, thousands of ideas must be gathered from all types of people who would be associated with the hotel as guests, operators, or suppliers. From this myriad of lesser ideas the architect prepares his master plan. Within his mind there is going on a constant evaluation and selection of ideas that are appropriate to the unconscious ideal that is directing his thinking. From these thousands of ideas must come the complete idea for a hotel that would be a prosperous enterprise.

This chapter is devoted to the morphological method of acquiring and synthesizing an unlimited number of ideas relative to any diffuse problem situation, and to the preparation of morphological charts indicating the relationships that need to be seen as the basis for a good solution.

Much vigorous argument is heard concerning the relative merits of the individual versus the group production of ideas. This is a pointless argument, to a morphologist, as any idea, no matter what might have been its source, will fit into the morphological pattern. For example, a restaurant man of my acquaintance developed an entirely new type of operation, based upon the suggestion of the laundry driver that cared for his cafe linens.

## 1. Avoid Scarcity of Ideas in the Midst of Plenty

### *Why are ideas so hard to get?*

The flow of ideas from the members of a group is often disappointingly small for two primary reasons, (1) a lack of motivation, and (2) the fear of consequences that may result from the submission of ideas.

The strongest motivation known to man is the desire to achieve his own potential, to be creative. You are often not creative because of the blocks that you impose upon yourself. You frustrate yourself, and suffer, because of these blocks.

### *Freedom of expression is paramount*

You will remember that in the family illustration given in the previous chapter nobody told the group what *he* thought the problems were. The leader simply *asked*. In this way, any prejudice was entirely eliminated. Complete freedom of expression was made both easy and pleasant. Following the private synthesis, by the leader, of all problem elements presented, the total family problem would be seen in stereo—from everybody's point of view *at one time*. No problem in the home, on the job, or between nations is too complicated for the morphological approach.

### *Anonymity—the key to truth*

To assist each member of the family to communicate exactly what he had in his mind, all ideas were written on small cards, only *one* idea to a card. All problems that any member could think of that might, in any way, be interfering with family happiness were submitted. No name was signed on any card. All ideas were kept completely separated from any personal identification. The leader of the family meeting summarized the cards and determined, from the pieces that had been submitted, what the *real* problems of the family were.

At the second family meeting, these problems were presented one at a time. Anonymous suggestions for solutions to the problems were written on cards by the family. The leader once again summarized and synthesized the ideas, and then prepared a brief written paper presenting the objective, the problems, and the solutions.

### *Anonymity stimulates creativity*

The expression of ideas will always be inhibited if there is fear of reprisal for being connected with some suggestions that might be taken as a reflection of the ability or the attitude of some member of an organization. On many occasions, anonymous replies provide the only means of gathering the information needed to solve some delicate or complex problem.

## 2. Use All of Your Sources of Ideas

### *Ideas come from knowledge*

Rain drops form because tiny dust particles in the air serve as nuclei, or centers, around which the surrounding vapor condenses. In a similar manner, an idea that you may have gleaned by reading or other experience, may serve as the nucleus for many ideas, in a nebulous state, that might otherwise drift right by without being noticed or caught. This is the reason why familiarity with up-to-date materials, methods, and information is such an important factor in personal growth.

### *Ideas come by accident*

Happy accidents, leading to notable creations, come only to those whose minds are filled with ideas. Stumbling onto an idea doesn't usually happen unless the hunter is out in the field searching for something—often not what he actually finds. Most so-called good luck is the result of determined effort. The lucky fisherman is often the one who casts his line in the stream most frequently.

Dr. E. O. Lawrence, late director of the University of California radiation laboratory who received the Nobel prize for his cyclotron, was described by Dr. Karl Compton of the Massachusetts Institute of Technology, as "the hardest worker that I ever knew."

### *Practice gaining new ideas*

Now and again you will come up with an original idea. If you will make a conscious effort to produce such ideas regularly it will eventually become a habit. If you will take just one more step and do something with the ideas immediately—at least to the extent of writing them down—the number of good ideas that come to you will be further increased.

One very simple way to start ideas generating, is to take a walk. The stirring up of purely physical energy will also stir up the mental energy that associates and develops ideas. Writers will often sit down at their typewriters and start typing whatever comes into their minds. After a while some pertinent, worthwhile, ideas begin to develop, and some good writing follows.

### *Ideas come from relaxation after tension*

Many inventors have told me that after a period of vigorous thought they relax temporarily, by letting their minds dwell on something else. Then suddenly—seemingly out of nowhere—the needed idea will come. Many research scientists have told me that after a series of solo efforts and vigorous "bull sessions" they have relaxed, and have dismissed the problem from their conscious mind. Sooner or later, the solution sought—or at least another part of the solution—would pop up in their mind. Professional idea men report that if they do not, by conscious effort, get the idea they are seeking they try to doze off. When they awaken, the idea they sought is usually available.

#### *Ideas come from thinking*

It is a good plan to take time out for doing nothing but thinking up ideas. Without a doubt, the most profitable stimulant to idea production is to ask questions—lots of questions.

As you think of a question—write it down. Soon you will have long lists of questions that will bring to your mind the way through a problem. More than stimulating your mind, questions also help it to function more efficiently. If you are trying to improve a product, ask questions about reducing cost, increasing its function, improving its performance, and increasing its salability. Two especially powerful questions to ask about any product or process that you wish to improve are, (1) *what* is this part for, and (2) *why* is it necessary in the first place?

### 3. Help—Don't Hinder Idea Production

#### *Ready-made idea starters*

Familiar, accessible publications, such as the Sears-Roebuck catalog and the Yellow Pages of the telephone book, make excellent check-lists. The strongest needs of man are listed in such publications. In addition to suggesting products to manufacture, the telephone book and the mail-order catalog suggest articles for writers and playwrights to develop. The advertisements in magazines and trade journals also offer many suggestions for ideas.

#### *Home-made idea starters*

The display man for a major drug concern always carries a small box in his car. Whenever he sees a good idea in his travels he notes it on a card and drops it in the box. Whenever he became stuck for a good new idea he would go to his box of "Idea

Starters." Shuffling through the cards would always give him more ideas than he could possibly use.

One of General Electric's most prolific inventors used announcements and articles concerning new materials as a never-ending source of suggestions for improving old products and for producing new ones. Frequently, a new material will make quite feasible the use of a design formerly found impractical.

### *How to put pressure on yourself*

Make a beginning. There is no better or simpler way. Once you have started something you feel under pressure until the project has been completed. The human personality has a very strong psychological urge to completion—so strong that it often sees things as complete when in reality they are not.

Setting deadlines or quotas will often put such a strong pressure on you that unexpectedly great results will be achieved. I frequently assign myself more pages to write in a day than seems possible of accomplishment. Under this pressure, ideas will merge and concepts be seen and understood, so that I often achieve my goal. There is something about setting goals, just a little above expectations, that stretches out achievements.

Large goals excite the imagination by providing a challenge. Building one hundred airplanes next week, if you have been building one hundred each week for the past year, provides no challenge. When the protection of our country demanded one thousand airplanes per week our only hope was to use creative imagination, and we produced the planes.

### *Getting ideas from other individuals*

One highly successful creative designer, in a manufacturing plant near Long Beach, California, has profited a great deal by making use of the desire of most people to try to meet a challenge. When this engineer was stopped by the lack of an idea needed in some design, he formed the habit of making a simple sketch outlining the problem and then posting it on a small bulletin board near his desk. As his colleagues passed his desk they would notice the sketch, and try to add a few lines or notes indicating a possible solution.

Many concerns are now seeking to gain ideas from their entire organization by means of suggestion systems. The key to the effective suggestion system is the flow of ideas and criticisms up from the workers, as well as down from the bosses.

### *Getting new ideas from old ones*

Checklists—suggesting new forms of old ideas, changes, modifications—are highly successful in spurring the questioning spirit. One distinct variation of the checklist is known as "attribute listing," developed by Professor Robert T. Crawford of the University of Nebraska. In this procedure the attributes of the various parts are listed and possible variations suggested. The attribute of the shank of the screw-driver is to transmit the torque applied to the handle, to the head of the screw. One possible variation is to make the shank *square,* so that a wrench may be applied to it, thereby increasing the possible torque.

What may seem to be a new idea may have originated from something observed ten or more years previously. When seen in some new light, an old idea gains new significance. Major concerns, such as Westinghouse and General Electric, say that most of today's products could just as well have been made ten years ago—if somebody had simply thought of them.

### *New ideas come from combination*

The *insight* that comes to a person is simply an intuitive synthesis of ideas into new relationships. Many groups of ideas are brought together entirely unconsciously. Some form of stimulus is desirable to broaden and to accelerate accidental intuition.

A "Design Synthesis Group" under the direction of William J. J. Gordon, formerly at the Arthur D. Little Company of Cambridge, Massachusetts, carries on a process that may be called psycho-synthesis. By this is meant the bringing of the individual intuitional powers of six or seven men into a group intuition. Then, as if a single person, the group will conceive and bring out inventions.

***Use of the morphological chart for solo or group ideation***

The ideas themselves are but the beginning of the creative process. What is done with the ideas after they have been produced is equally as important as the ideas themselves. Most of the idea-producing plans concentrate on the production of ideas as an end in itself. Morphology stresses the finding of all possible relationships of ideas.

Let us take the two-column morphological chart used to indicate the plan used in finding applications for use in this book, (page vi). By the simple addition of the ten sub-objectives of this book, the total number of relationships between the three parameters is four hundred and ninety.

| *Sub-Objectives* | *Areas of Living* | *Problem Systems* |
|---|---|---|
| A. SATISFACTION OF HUMAN NEEDS | A. SELF | A. FINANCE |
| B. DEVELOPMENT OF PERSONALITY | B. FAMILY | B. DISCIPLINE |
| C. ACHIEVEMENT OF OPEN-MINDEDNESS | C. OCCUPATION | C. HEALTH |
| D. IMPROVEMENT OF HUMAN RELATIONS | D. COMMUNITY | D. ESTEEM-POWER |
| E. UTILIZATION OF ALL APTITUDES | E. COUNTRY | E. EDUCATION |
| F. TOTAL THINKING | F. WORLD | F. COMMUNICATION |
| G. CONFIDENT PROB-LEM SOLVING | G. CHURCH | G. RECREATION |
| H. DEPENDABLE DE-CISION MAKING | | |
| I. A WORKING PHILOSOPHY | | |
| J. ACHIEVEMENT OF CREATIVE IMAGE | | |

## 4. Don't Be a Slave to Habits and Customs

***Freedom from prejudice***

If the solving of a problem involves personalities, or the protection of "empires" within an organization, it is very difficult to overcome the effect of prejudice on the ideas offered. As mentioned earlier, the only way for complete and honest expression of ideas to be had, on controversial problems, is for strict anonymity to be preserved.

The widely used procedure of "brainstorming" is most effective, usually when there is a relative evenness of "rank" among the participants. The president of a bank would probably not be in the same brainstorming session as the girls who post the checks. Yet, if the prejudices of the various members of an organization can be prevented from influencing the ideas expressed, it is of tremendous value to have an entire organization working side by side on a problem of vital concern to all.

### *Treatment of ideas*

Ideas expressed orally by a group may be taken down in shorthand by a secretary, they may be written on a blackboard, or they may be tape recorded. In group ideation such as this, there is, of course, no anonymity, which will cause many good ideas not to be expressed.

When such a controversial problem as how to reorganize a company is under discussion the basic ideas needed will be obtained more quickly and more easily when strict anonymity is had. The simplest way yet devised is to have each idea written down on a small card, approximately 2.5 by 3.0 inches in size.

After the ideas from a brainstorming session dealing with either a relatively simple problem, or one phase of a complex problem, have been recorded, they are then screened in accordance with the understanding or prejudices of the screeners. The screened list is then handed to the one who will use it. A brainstorm panel has finished its job when it has submitted a screened list of ideas. Pointing out the significance of groups of ideas is not considered to be the responsibility of a brainstorm panel. From six to twelve persons are the usual number of members.

When a complex problem—of the nature appropriate to the morphological treatment—is to be solved, ideas from as many persons as possible are gathered, each idea on a separate card. The morphologist directing work on the problem will synthesize all of the ideas presented into a display called a morphological chart—or morphologram. From this dynamic chart—so-called because the columns of ideas actually move up and down (see types in Appendix)—all possible relationships of the various components will be indicated.

### *What is a good idea?*

An act, or an idea, may rightfully be evaluated only in terms of the objective being sought by the person who proposes the idea. You may not evaluate my ideas in terms of your objective —unless we have a mutual objective that is recognized and accepted by both of us. Judging and evaluation are absolutely essential for any organization that wishes to continue to exist. It is when *premature* judging of an idea takes place that damage is done. You would not judge a painting that was only half completed. Neither should you judge an idea until it can be seen as a part of some complete structure or plan.

### *A common objective can eliminate prejudice*

When both the proponent of an idea and its evaluator have the same objective in mind then prejudice may be eliminated. Modern artists claim as the objective for their "art" the expression of their inner feelings. Regardless of how awful some artists may feel, if my objective for art is the nostalgic primitive of Grandma Moses, I am not qualified to evaluate their creations.

The wrong objective, or the wrong problem, whether held by the person proposing an idea or the one receiving it, renders true evaluation impossible. If you were thinking about moving a mountain of dirt as quickly as possible and had concluded that larger trucks was the answer, any idea that would make possible the faster movement of the trucks already in use would not be rated highly.

The waitress who snatches away your half emptied plate, when your eyes are momentarily diverted, is moving straight toward *her* objective of getting you out of your seat as soon as possible, so that another tip might be forthcoming. *Your* objective, that of satisfying your hunger, is now further off. If the primary objective of a school administrator is to keep the public contented with things as they are, he will then be opposed to anything which might require a little public adjustment.

### *New ideas need kindness and loving care*

New ideas are like the young, tender shoots that push through the ground. They must be treated gently, protected, and nourished. I can well remember the feel of an icy blast on my face as I stepped out of the kitchen door of my Massachusetts home on a winter's morning. My reaction was to cover up a little more completely. An idea that meets with an icy blast is also painful to its producer. He also tends to cover up—by withholding other ideas that may be very good as well as being different. It is far easier to ridicule a good idea than it is to adjust to it. Sometimes it is better not to express your choice ideas in too unfriendly circumstances.

Moreover, an idea that is not acted upon is often lost forever. If it does not seem appropriate to express an idea audibly, then act by writing it down on a card and tossing it into an idea bank. You will be greatly surprised at how often one of those deposited ideas will adequately fill some later need.

### *Freedom from the restrictions of custom*

There are two types of problem activities. One is to modify an existing solution in an effort to bring about some improvement, the other is to go way back to the fundamentals of the problem itself. While other car manufactures were trying to increase the sale of new cars by tacking on absurd and functionless fins, George Mason, president of American Motors, considered anew the basic objectives of an automobile. His successor, George Romney, did much to popularize the compact car by asking such pointed questions as, "Why does a one hundred pound woman need a four thousand pound car to drive four blocks to a supermarket to get a one pound loaf of bread?" Mason and Romney both saw real needs, set up appropriate objectives, and then solved the problems in the way of reaching their objectives.

George Mason and Charles Nash saw that a unit construction of body and chassis would both save weight and give a safer car that could be built at a lower cost. General Motors, with its huge investment in separate frame and body plants, rejected the unitized construction until forced—in spite of itself—into the compact car market. It is quite possible that all of the ideas that were so successfully applied by George Mason at American Motors, had been suggested—and squelched—at General Motors, Ford and Chrysler.

### *Lowering resistance to new ideas*

New ideas are usually resisted by most people. Some persons are more versatile in seeing the purpose behind new ideas than are others. Resistance to your ideas will be sharply reduced if you will first take the time to clarify your objective—and gain acceptance of it—before offering ideas for the solution of a problem *that had not yet occurred to the other person.*

The sales force of a Los Angeles concern flatly refused to have anything to do with a revised sales program proposed by the sales manager. An outside consultant was brought in who asked the salesmen for ideas that would increase their commissions. The salesmen liked this objective—it was theirs. From the large number of ideas the salesmen gave him the consultant prepared a new program that was enthusiastically received and approved by the entire sales force. This program was almost exactly the same as the one proposed by the sales manager.

### *Habits may be either good or bad*

Habits are time and energy savers. They will often save you from the expenditure of excessive mental effort. They become harmful when they rigidize your thinking to such an extent as to make you insensitive to the entrance of something new into the situation. One very profitable habit is to ask periodically, "Why am I doing this job in this way?" A really courageous person will ask, "Why is this job necessary?"

## 5. Use Ideas on Hand to Suggest Others Without Limit

### *Look for* new *adaptations of* old *ideas*

There are thousands of new uses for old ideas, just waiting for someone to think of them. Certain people, who have what we call imagination, seem to see these new uses intuitively, without consciously trying. Many other persons would see those new uses if given just a little nudge in the right direction. In this section will be shown some ways in which this nudge may be given.

Had Professor Langley made a *complete* list of the relatively few known methods of causing a body to move through the air, he might have thought of using rockets (jets), and have succeeded in making his plane fly, when his steam engine failed. Rockets have been known for a thousand years, airplanes have been flying for more than fifty years, but only within the past five years have commercial jet airliners been in use.

A child's toy from Russia consisted of a doll with two heads—a princess at one end and a peasant at the other. There was a reversible dress appropriate to the character in view. American children were not much interested in this doll. But when a manufacturer made one of the doll heads that of Little Red Riding-hood, and the other head that of a wolf, putting a music box inside that played, "Who's Afraid of the Big Bad Wolf?"—SALES SKYROCKETED.

Adhesive strips across the corners of snapshots have been used for mounting for many years. Glue or paste has also so served. The adhesive strips spoiled the effect, and the glue frequently damaged the snapshot when removed. One ingenious chap put adhesive on *both* surfaces of Scotch tape, thereby eliminating the defects of both of the former methods.

### *Producing new ideas by forming associations of old ideas*

In a discussion of possible means of acquiring new ideas with Dr. William Shockley—recipient of the Nobel prize for his work on transistors and other solid state devices—the scientist stressed the importance of the *association* of ideas. Dr. Shockley pointed out that a man with two ideas relative to an invention can create in two ways, but that a man with three pertinent ideas can offer six arrangements of the three ideas, or six possible inventions. Most of those profitable ideas which cause you to say, "Now why didn't I think of that?" are of this association-of-old-ideas type.

### *How to take the guess-work out of seeing idea relationships*

Suppose that you were the manager of the shipping department of a firm with a wide range of products and markets. How many different types of containers could you think of, off hand? Do you think you could list as many as four thousand? This would be a very simple task if you used the method illustrated by the morphological chart that follows.

*Design Characteristics for Containers*

| I. PRODUCT | II. MATERIALS | III. CARRIER | IV. DESTINATION |
|---|---|---|---|
| Solid | Wood | Private Car | Local |
| Liquid (Neutral) | Aluminum | Company Truck | Within State |
| Gaseous | Steel | Commercial Truck | Out of State |
| Radioactive | Glass | Train | Out of U.S. |
| Liquid (Corrosive) | Plywood | Airplane | Space |
| Temperature Sensitive | Paper | Boat | Homes |
| Food | Plastic | Space Ship | Stores |
| Alive | Lead | Missile | Military |

You will note that there are listed but thirty-two separate elements, if they are considered but one at a time. However, if one item of each category—four at one time—are seen as one relationship, there are then more than four thousand different types of boxes suggested.

Take for example the transportation of goldfish from your

store by retail customers. You then have the problem of providing some inexpensive means by which your customer can carry his fish home. Referring to the container chart, one suggested possibility is: *Alive, Plastic, Private Car, Home.* This suggests a small plastic bag with the fish and the water *sealed* up inside; the customer carrying it home in his own car.

It has been found that a flat bottom plastic bag, about one-half full of water, will provide enough air to keep a fish alive for several days. Being tightly sealed there is no danger of leakage, and the parcel may be carried in a shopping bag or laid on the seat of the car.

This simple chart directs the attention to many things that can make safe delivery more likely, and also suggests many ways in which shipping costs can be reduced. A glass container would be adequate for a corrosive liquid that was going to be transported by company truck, or private car, but not safe for shipment by train. The destination is an important consideration because of the specific laws governing interstate shipments. Some of these regulations relative to packaging make such a difference in shipping costs as to warrant different containers for various destinations.

## 6. Utilize to the Maximum Your Unlimited Imagination

### *What is imagination?*

Imagination is the act of forming a concept of what is not actually present to the senses. In its essence, imagination is seeing relationships. It is the bringing together of two or more ideas to form a new idea. Assume that you have acquired ten thousand different ideas in your lifetime. The number of possible combinations of these ideas would be so great as to exceed in number the total of all the grains of sand on all the beaches of the world. Getting a paltry million ideas does not, then, seem to be such a very difficult ask.

### *Imagination brings about miracles*

To make use of your wealth of ideas you must either bring them to your conscious mind, and relate them consciously to your problem; or you must submerge your problem in your subconscious, then let the problem move around in your idea storage picking up those ideas it needs to produce some solutions. The details of submerging an idea in your subconscious are treated in Chapter 9. In this section we are simply pointing out the unlimited possibilities of your imagination—the unknown depths of your creative power.

### *Imagination is questioning*

Imagination begins with the asking of questions—either consciously or subconsciously. Imagination asks the questions, and sets up the objectives, toward which logical reasoning laboriously plods.

"I am a thinking rebel," was the way one successful inventor described himself, "I am constantly asking *why* is it necessary to do it in this way."

### *Take the chains off your imagination*

Even though imagination is often frowned upon we need to decondition ourselves, and let our imagination explode. "I look right around me for things to improve. I continually ask myself, does this thing satisfy me now? I have an urge to one hundred per cent efficiency, to make it better, cheaper, faster." These were the comments of a very successful inventor.

### *Use planned imagination*

*Planned* imagination means to acquire *all* possible ideas relative to a problem or situation. It means to be free from prejudice, to see ideas in all possible relationships. Freedom from prejudice does not mean the absence of judgment, it means only the "suspension" of judgment—until all available ideas have been acquired and synthesized.

Planned imagination makes use of the fact that it is from individuals faced with a problem that the best solutions are to be found. Morphological creativity, as developed in this book, utilizes planned imagination in the acquisition and synthesizing of ideas into solutions of problems.

That no idea has ever been generated except in a single mind is a true statement, but one that is often horribly misused. It is frequently taken to mean that no group of persons can ever create anything, and that creative people should work independently. The stimulus for the generation of an idea usually comes from some other person. It comes from something that the other person has said or done, or through the recognition of some other person's need. It is very often the case that a single idea given in a group discussion proves to be just the idea that was needed by some member of the group to crystallize a phase of his own thinking.

## 7. Utilize the Broad Principles of Ideation

### *Two basic types of ideation*

Although the number of ways of gathering ideas seems to be almost without limit, there are in reality but two *basic* procedures. Ideas may be had by the acquisition of new individual ideas, or may be *produced* by the synthesis—or association—of available ideas.

Psychological research is just beginning to uncover some of the elements of the creative process—that is the intellectual operations that go on during the creative act. There is therefore, as yet, no set formula for the production of ideas.

Brainstorming, Attribute Listing, and G.E. Input-Output technics, are perhaps the most successful methods for the simple acquisition of ideas for specific, clearly-expressed problems. The Gordon Design-Synthesis method appears to be the best for use by a carefully selected, highly trained group who are concerned with the solution of a specific technical problem involving invention of a product. Where the problem is controversial and one of complexity, and initial vagueness, morphological creativity has many unique advantages.

### *What is the objective being sought?*

When the investigation of a problem goes as far back as the basic objective, it is often found that the product involved is not the best solution of the real problem. If the true objective is the improvement of health conditions through the elimination of flies, the problem of how to prevent their breeding is a far better one to solve than how to produce more effective fly traps.

Going back to the basic objective, and visualizing the problems that should be solved, will stimulate the flow of many more ideas than will the consideration of the limited goal of improving an existing fly trap.

### *How to treat ideas*

Ideas should be treated with kindness and respect. Nothing is gained by making an idea fight for its very life just as soon as it is born. It is very easy to squelch an idea which has intuitively been produced: for, even to its proud parent, the steps by which the idea was developed are very often not all apparent.

If any new idea is received, make every possible effort to fill in the gaps in understanding so that any values that may exist in the idea will not be lost—even though the idea as presented may not be usable. This kind of treatment encourages the off-beat thinker—who usually has the novel ideas—to suggest others.

# 3

## HOW TO CONTROL IDEAS

***Maximum creativity requires much general knowledge***

A great many scientists of national reputation have told me that when entering into the study of a problem area they did not want to know too much about what others had done in the field. Their concern was that they might be enticed into a direction that would prove to be wrong. The scientists feared that heavy proportion of ideas of the same general nature might cause their importance to be overestimated. This could result in some very significant, though divergent fact, being overlooked.

This rather prevalent viewpoint has given me some concern because it tends to avoid looking for relationships, rather than seeking them. There is little doubt that this isolationship tendency is retarding our national scientific and cultural development.

### 1. Be the Master Not the Slave of Your Ideas

***The power of intuition***

On many occasions, great scientists and inventors have very strongly emphasized their dependence upon their intuition, or subconscious, for what is popularly called "break-throughs."

The exposure to extensive amounts of the work of other investigators can so saturate the conscious, logical mind that the products of intuition, the subconscious mind, are blotted out.

This need not happen, however. All knowledge, all ideas, and all things are ultimately related, and in an infinite number of ways. The problem, then, is not one of neglecting the work of others, but in synthesizing it with one's own experience.

### *Don't be afraid of ideas*

Most ideas will never gain the upper hand unless an attempt is made to evaluate them against a non-existent standard, *as they are being acquired.* Ideas become troublesome only when they are not in harmony with what one believes.

### *Organized ideas are under control*

Two hundred books piled in the middle of the living room floor would be disturbing to all users of the room. The same books classified on the library shelves have a positive effect. There are many ways in which the books may be organized on the shelves. They may be classified by author, alphabetically, by subject, or by numerical sequence of their acquisition. In the sequential system each book is given a number without regard to content. The actual classification being done with cards in a file.

The organization of ideas should be in terms of the basic objective sought, because the basic objective determines the problems, which in turn establishes the plan of the idea display.

### *Provide a parking lot for incoming ideas*

At a football game in the Pasadena Rose Bowl, where in 1961 Long Beach became the national junior college champions, the parking was especially well handled. The automobiles were parked *as they came* in neat rows and sections. The main concern was to get as many cars parked as quickly as possible, with as rapid egress after the game as the exit roads could handle.

Let your imagination operate freely for a moment, and assume that Honest Jack, the used car dealer, has purchased all of the cars from the owners during the game. They are now his to do with as he wishes.

As the cars are now arranged, compacts, limousines, station wagons, and campers of all types and conditions are indiscriminately mixed up. The dealer has several alternative display plans. He may group the cars by make or sales price, or he may use a combination of the two. He is able to arrange the cars *at his own rate,* and do a good job.

Suppose that Honest Jack had attempted to arrange the cars in a selling array *as they came into the parking area.* The confusion, inefficiency, and traffic jam would have been such as to have prevented all but the first few cars to have been parked prior to game time.

### *A simple plan for controlling ideas*

If rapidly incoming ideas are arranged as they are received, the idea traffic jam that results raises a strong demand for some kind of relief. The easiest way is to shunt off into discard any ideas which will not fit into familiar slots. The novel ideas, the ones that have inherent possibilities for unique and better solutions are lost.

In handling ideas, take a lesson from the automobile parking example. Write each idea *as it appears* on an individual card. I have found that 2.5 by 3 inch cards used horizontally are ideal.

Now I park these ideas, sometimes as many as several thousand. The cards are arranged on a counter or table in blocks of twelve, in three columns of four cards each, just as I happen to pick them up from the receiving box. As in the case of the parked cars, I have room mentally to pass up and down among the ideas. There is no confusion in my mind or pressure to organize the cards in any special way. The ideas are now in a condition to be absorbed into my subconscious mind, there to be related to the wealth of other ideas already on deposit. There is no pressure, because there is as yet no classification of the ideas.

The classification of the ideas is not inherent in the ideas themselves but in the *basic objectives* which may be determined from the ideas acquired. The distinction is a nice one but is highly important. *There are no problems without an objective.* If the objective of a farmer is to plant a field of corn, it is not his problem if a carload of wheat does not arrive. On the other hand, if the drive gear on the corn-planter is broken, this poses a problem which the farmer must solve. The solution of the wheat problem by an Air Force air lift means nothing to the corn problem. The sequence of events on problem solving (one that is often mixed up) is: first, establish the objective; second, determine the problems in the way of the objective; third, find solutions to the problems.

As a business consultant I may find a company whose immediate objective is to make enough profit to make it possible to stay in business. At the outset I do not know what the problems are that must be solved; so I ask everybody within reach who is in any way concerned with the profits what they think the problems are. I do not *pretend* that I know what the problems are. I admit that I do not, and ask the people *with* the problems to tell me what they are. I receive the ideas, usually on cards, and handle them as described.

## 2. Invest Your Ideas at Compound Interest

### *Profit is the reward of risk*

An idea in a cage is like a silver dollar buried in the ground. Both are safe, but neither produces anything. The dollar, when invested in seed that is planted, cared for, and harvested, may return a profit of one hundred dollars. Admittedly, there was a *chance* that the seed might not grow to maturity, but it was a *certainty* that there would be no crop if the dollar had not been spent for seed.

### *An idea is never used up*

An idea is a wonderful kind of seed. It may be planted again and again, and is always still ready for further use. An idea is like a catalyst in a chemical reaction. Without it the reaction will not take place. But the idea is not consumed. It is always available for further use.

The sun has been radiating tremendous amounts of energy for billions of years at a rate that would have consumed annually a layer of coal three thousand miles thick. It has now been shown that the carbon of the sun is used only as a catalyst. Hydrogen is used up as fuel but not the carbon.

### *Henry Ford's great idea*

Nearly fifty years ago Henry Ford was given the idea that he could sell a lot more cars if the employees that made the automobiles could buy them. This meant raising the minimum daily wage from about two dollars to five dollars. Although Detroit predicted failure, the phenomenal success of the Ford Motor Company justified this revolutionary idea.

Better decisions are always made when it is recognized that the greatest urge of any person is the expression of his own potentialities. Such a startling raise in wages for so many people who had barely been getting by, made many personal developments possible, that had formerly not been experienced.

### *A simple idea worth one billion dollars*

It has been known since the time of the Pilgrim's landing at Provincetown, Massachusetts, that some substances would readily conduct electricity while others would not. But it was only in 1948 that Bardeen, Brattain, and Shockley announced the application of semi-conductors to transistors.

A semi-conductor is a substance such as silicon or germanium that is normally a non-conductor but which becomes a conductor of fairly low resistance with the application of sufficient potential.

Among its many applications a transistor the size of a pea can replace a standard three-electrode vacuum tube. It has an unlimited life, and uses but one-millionth the power of an equivalent glass or metal envelope vacuum tube. Just think of the great returns from the simple idea of semi-conductors. Relays may be put in submarine telephone cables with the assurance of many years of trouble-free operation. Tiny self-contained hearing aids that fit entirely in the ear itself are now available.

### *How to have a better world overnight*

If you have the feeling that you are working with a pretty selfish group of people, set aside a day in which you make every effort to give away ideas that might help someone to do his job just a little bit easier or better. You will be surprised how your associates have improved, and how generous they have become. People *do* like to give as well as to receive.

## 3. Synthesize All Available Ideas Before Evaluating Any of Them

### *Creativity is the synthesis of ideas*

Most ideas are the result of combinations. Even the most creative thinker will evolve very few completely new ideas. Synthesis is thus the very essence of creativity.

To be creative the ability to synthesize is required. Synthesis means the making of generalizations from the combinations of ideas. If the synthesis of elements is done vicariously, without bringing things together physically, the process is called imagination. Synthesis and creative activity are synonymous.

Expressed in a slightly different way, the essence of the creative process is combination plus imagination.

### *Synthesis—the establishment of relationships*

Synthesis involves a search for unifying concepts. Related ideas are always more helpful than ideas considered independently.

Synthesis is like putting together the pieces of a puzzle. The significance of any one piece lies in its relationship to the *completed* ensemble.

The association of ideas, which is synthesis, is a process by which imagination fuses together memory and new experiences.

### *Creative synthesis is a step into the new*

The creative mind is bold, courageous. It can synthesize original designs without attempting to analyze each idea before expressing the product. The test of the successfulness of the step into the new lies in the logical evaluation, or its application and verification. Creative synthesis, then, is an intuitive process.

### *Insight—the subconscious recognition of ideational synthesis*

Insight is an imaginative way of learning or problem solving, in contrast to the blind process of trial-and-error. The probable results are looked for and an element of evaluation is inherent in insight.

### *A clear objective stimulates synthesis*

A common error is to attempt to depend on *isolated* facts in making decisions. If one examines all available facts with enough care he will be able to establish the basic objective. With a clear purpose in view synthesis will be accelerated. If you have a limited objective of driving a nail in the wall, and find yourself without a hammer, it will be a very simple matter to reject a sponge in favor of a door knob.

Energy put into a bowling ball gives it the momentum that carries it down the alley for a strike. Even though the intuitive association of synthesis might seem to be automatic, it too depends, to a very large extent, on the *accumulated* mental energy. In some unknown manner, an idea full of kinetic energy seems to swish around in the subconscious. During its vigorous journey it bumps into many other ideas, some of which it retains in new and helpful relationships. So far we can't prove to you intellectually that it will occur; it is something that you will have to try for yourself.

A clear objective, which helps to release the ideational energy referred to, also makes more likely the recognition of the universal aspects of a set of accumulated ideas.

### *The stimulation of concept formation*

The process of synthesis works far better for those whose minds are well stocked with ideas and whose imagination is free. Improvement of creative ability requires the constant accumulation of knowledge and the improvement of the ability to synthesize ideas into new associations.

The creative thinker is a master in thinking by analogy. Seeing helpful resemblances between the parking and arranging of cars for sale, and the acquisition and display of ideas is an example of a helpful analogy. Visualizing automobile traffic as a flowing stream, like a river, suggests the removal of debris, increasing the size of the "pipe," the erection of bridges and many other ideas that readily come to mind.

Concentration will naturally make efforts to synthesize ideas much more fruitful. This may be readily appreciated if concentration is seen as relaxing, by the elimination of irrelevant ideas —not as an increased strain.

### *The evaluation of ideas*

The evaluation of an individual idea may properly be made *only* in terms of the total synthesis of all ideas available that are pertinent to the objective sought. Alertness is important because not every idea at hand is relevant, even though it may be a very clever one.

Testing of an idea by actual application is, of course, the surest form of evaluation. One important problem in evaluation is *when* to test. Certainly it can not be evaluated until after the basic objective is clearly established, and the problems to be solved are recognized. A very clever idea that does not solve, or help to solve a problem, in the way of attaining the objective, is not a good idea.

## 4. Determine the Total Meaning of Synthesized Ideas

### *The meaning of an idea*

The Oxford Dictionary defines *Meaning* as that which is *intended* to be, or *actually* is expressed or indicated: significance.

In this chapter, dealing with the control of ideas, we need to know what ideas mean. Not by themselves, but when all available ideas pertinent to a given situation are synthesized into a small enough number of larger ideas to be taken in at one time, with all relationships being felt.

### *The development of meaning*

The development of meaning involves the extension and the multiplication of relationships. We give meaning to a word, not by endlessly repeating the same word, but by structuring around the word of unknown meaning many other words whose meanings are clearly understood. It is out of the integrated relationships among these other words that the desired meaning is given to the unknown word.

The purpose of this section is to demonstrate how the same process is applicable to the determination of the significance of an idea.

### *An hydro-electric analogy*

When thinking through any problem, particularly one of a rather unfamiliar type, making use of simple analogies is always very helpful.

Example: In the search for much needed power, public utilities are investigating every possible source, including water. Thousands of ideas have been acquired from many groups of people who will be affected by any new utilization of water resources.

To gain the maximum meaning from these ideas it is necessary to synthesize them in such a way that their total meaning, the significance of all interrelationships, will be perceived.

Let us assume that the individual concepts may be displayed in three categories, or parameters: *Finances, Water Supply,* and *Water Uses*. Each of these parameters has from two to seven components, or parts, as shown on chart 3—1.

One of the components of *Water Supply* is *Total Useful Head.* How important is this particular synthesis of ideas? While the

Chart 3—1

THE CHOICE OF A WATER SUPPLY

| *FINANCES* | *WATER SUPPLY* | *WATER USES* |
|---|---|---|
| COSTS | TOTAL QUANTITY | POWER |
| INCOME | STEADINESS OF SUPPLY | IRRIGATION |
| | TOTAL USEFUL HEAD | HOME |
| | LEGAL RIGHTS IN EFFECT | INDUSTRY |
| | CHOICES OF SOURCES | MINING |
| | STORAGE | RECREATION |
| | DISTRIBUTION | TRANSPORTATION |

available head of water is, of course, an essential element in the development of hydro-electric power, it can not be the sole basis for a choice of water supply. Any one of the other components might be the determining factor.

A large supply of water at a relatively low head might be quite satisfactory for irrigation or domestic purposes but very unsatisfactory for a source of hydro-electric power.

The variety of uses to which the available water can be put may well make the selection of one source with a lower head preferable to another source, with a much greater head that is primarily of concern to the generation of electric power.

The storage of water could have an undesirable effect on the stream fishing, but sportsmen might not object to this if a new lake were formed that made possible boating and swimming as well as fishing.

### *Synthesis as an intellectual operation*

Hour by hour we are all receiving hundreds of stimuli through our various senses. Our mind must include a fantastically complicated computing machine to handle all the incoming traffic. The output of this "computing machine" is what is meant by perception. Perception is the final image of what takes place when one meaningfully engages himself with objects, persons, and events in his environment.

The existence of too many perceptual blocks, those things that prevent a person from getting a true picture of the world in which he must operate, will prevent that person from being an innovator.

Not only is synthesis dependent on a perceptual process, reacting to outside stimuli, but also on a conceptual process. A concept is that which is conceived in the mind as the result of productive imagination. The relating of the two is inherent in the intuitive process.

## 5. Avoid Prejudice by Synthesizing Ideas Before Analyzing Problems

***Why and when to analyze***

Creativity involves both the synthesis of ideas and the analysis of problems. In the solution of complex problems both aspects of creativity are utilized.

When a problem is broken down into its elements, solutions are often immediately suggested. This is referred to as the analysis of a gross problem into sub-problems. Personal problems, those involving human relations, are usually complex and to obtain solutions must be broken down into component elements.

All of the above customary comments on problem analysis are quite true. But, because they do not convey the *whole* truth, many poor solutions of problems are proposed and accepted.

To be safe, it is most essential, before any analysis is attempted, *to be certain that it is the TOTAL problem that is being analyzed.* After a chart similar to, but usually more complex than chart 3—1 of the preceding section, has been prepared *by synthesis,* then it is proper and unprejudiced to separate the total problem into its *natural* segments.

After the problem has been broken down into its parts, it will usually be found that the solution of some of these parts can be had from experience. There is danger in breaking down a problem into independent bits, thus losing sensitivity to new relationships and new conditions that may have arisen since a similar situation was experienced by the problem solver.

If the evaluation of incoming ideas—as well as any attempted analysis of the problem—is deferred until the "total-problem" chart has been constructed, additional and novel ideas essential to creative solutions will be submitted.

### *Problem formulation precedes problem analysis*

If the problem at hand is specific, limited in scope, and capable of solution on the basis of experience, *perhaps* finding the solution may commence with chopping up the problem into little bits. This is a limited concept of the broad meaning of analysis. Analysis may include synthesis, but this is not the meaning usually had in discussions of problem solving. In order to be understood by most readers, we will ourselves use the limited concept of analysis, that of separating a whole into its parts.

Analysis can be made only after there is a complete problem to analyze, for how can you take to pieces something that you now neither see nor comprehend?

An illustration of decision making, given in detail in Chapter 9, illustrates how a premature analysis of a manufacturing problem first based on production and test data alone could have resulted in a costly mistake. When the ideas from the sales department were included in the problem structure, quite another decision was made.

During the stage of problem formulation the open minded viewpoint should be maintained. Research activities should be free and uninfluenced by preconceived solutions. Research may be defined as a course of critical or scientific *inquiry*—as a time of questioning.

The process of research is to collect the pieces of an *unknown* problem, and to put the pieces together so that the problem may be recognized. Then the problem may be taken to pieces.

## 6. Be Sure that the "King" Value is the Center of All Evaluations Made

### *What to do with 10,000 ideas*

In most morphological charts there will be hundreds, often thousands of associations comprising parts of the total problem.

The careful, or even cursory, consideration of all possible problem elements is quite impossible.

Being confronted with such a large number of pieces is so overwhelming as to be frightfully frustrating. In normal situations the mind will not bring up for consideration more elements than the same mind wants to consider. Although far from including the total problem, the number of elements the mind of itself brings up is enough to satisfy the mind. It is content to work with the incomplete picture if it puts together all of the parts of the problem it has at hand. There is an intuitive rationalization to the effect that the mind can't handle any more elements, so why look for them?

The difficulty in evaluation comes from a tendency to consider all elements of the problem as being of equal significance. If the elements are all given a rank order, on some acceptable basis, then one can start at the top and go as far down the list as time, or other factors, permit.

The writer has received frantic communications from several engineers, and others, while in the process of solving problems by the morphological method being described.

### *What is the "King" value?*

I asked Dr. F. Zwicky of the California Institute of Technology, the man who introduced morphology to astronomy and to chemical propulsion in this country, what he himself did.

Dr. Zwicky's suggestion was, "Ask the question, what is the 'King' value, today, right now?"

By this Dr. Zwicky meant, what one objective is the most pressing, the one that above all others will, if achieved, indicate a successful solution of the problem of concern. The identification of this "King" value, and a keen appreciation of its stature, makes possible the elimination of enough irrelevant or minor elements so that it is possible to evaluate those remaining.

### *How use of the "King" value simplifies idea control*

In chart 3—1 there are ninety-eight possible combinations of the three parameters. While this quantity is not too many to evaluate we will assume that it is, and reduce the number of associations to be comprehended.

The "King" value is determined from the specifications of the problem. These specifications are sometimes directly stipulated, but often are derived from the data accumulated during research on the problem.

Let us say that in the hydro-electric power situation that the "King" value is an increase in available electric power. In the area served by the utility are several defense plants working on top priority projects. With an increase in power production being the one outstanding need, or value, being sought, the other possible uses of water listed become of relatively small significance. Here, too, the cost of development and the net income to the company are also of less than usual importance.

So far as the water supply is concerned, an adequate and steady supply with sufficient head, will be the components of major significance. Even the legal rights held by various interests will be set aside if their contributions to defense activities is considerably less than that which the power company would make with the added water.

There are always one or two values that are paramount in any situation, and their utilization in the selection of problem elements to stress will make good solutions probable.

The "King" value is, of course, always closely related to the basic objective.

## 7. Develop Internal Standards of Evaluation

### *The need for internal standards of evaluation*

Internal standards of evaluation are of importance only when vague problems involving original research are of concern. It will be the rare exception when there will not be some known standards for the external evaluation of any idea.

At times, however, when no external comparisons can be made, internal standards—even though not absolute—are very useful in narrowing the area of operations.

### *Evaluation means to judge the new in terms of the old*

It is a relatively simple matter to evaluate a new kind of room insulation. A direct comparison with the others on the market will suffice to establish the rank of the new insulation.

### *Evaluation without a known standard*

Suppose, on the other hand, that you had invented an erasing key for a typewriter, something that the world has needed for a long time. In this instance there is no outside "known" with which to compare, or evaluate. You will be forced to look at the various elements of the whole erasing process and to ask questions. Questions need to be asked such as, Why was this part made as it was? Just what does it accomplish? What changes might be made in the part so that it will perform its function better?

### *Internal evaluation in business research*

Another situation where internal standards of evaluation are useful is where the operation of an entire business is being studied. First, from ideas submitted, the basic objective of the business is established. Then the problems in the way of obtaining the objective are determined, and finally the ideas leading to their solutions are sought.

Ideas for solutions can be evaluated in terms of their contribution to the most desirable solutions. Other things being equal, a solution is most satisfactory when it solves a problem adequately, and at the same time introduces the fewest new difficulties to be cleared away.

After the solutions have been applied to the various problems, the results may then be compared with those obtained by other companies as they solved the same problems. The question may be raised by some reader, "Why not *start* with the best solution that anyone else has found and go on from there?"

The reason is that if the start is made from the problem fundamentals a better view of the real problem is had, and an entirely new solution may be produced.

# 4

## HOW TO THINK CREATIVELY

### *Creative talent is universal*

Creativity is a quality existing in all persons. The factors of creativity *seem* to vary from person to person both in the amount of initial deposit, and in the degree to which this potential is realized and developed. I say *seem* because nobody has as yet devised any measure that even purports to measure the extent of the creative potential of an individual. About all that has been *proved* is that the creative potential of any person is used very little, in comparison to possible achievement, and that creative ability—creative achievement—can be greatly developed through training and practice.

Creativity is universal in its fundamental structure in all of the arts and sciences. There is a single set of tools used by creative thinkers regardless of their lines of work. This may explain why Leonardo da Vinci could be so outstanding as a painter, sculptor, musician, scientist, inventor and engineer.

### *The fundamental problem of creativity is to release it*

You *can* be more creative, if you will. Every great writer was once an amateur. Every great inventor had to produce his first invention, often against vigorous opposition. Very often you will have to *gain* the opportunity to be creative. If you want to be creative you must expect to have to work for it. Since any person's basic potential remains the same from day to day, variations in his creativity are determined by energy changes.

## 1. Free the Frozen Assets of Your Mind

### *Preparation for creativity*

Start off with being open-minded, which means the willingness to *receive,* without immediate evaluation, all ideas submitted. Judgment should be suspended if prejudice, the greatest enemy of creativity, is to be avoided.

A concept that has become firmly fixed in your mind may often prove to be the strongest barrier to the acceptance of ideas that would lead to the development of a better concept.

One often overlooked requirement for creativity is that of getting a sufficient background of knowledge and experience so that new associations will be made. Luck, in creativity, is usually the result of investigators so steeping themselves in their problems that novel ideas experienced find sensitized spots to attach themselves, often being done subconsciously. The theory of gravity was conceived only when the apple fell on a prepared mind.

### *How to stimulate creativity*

The strong urge to accomplish something notable is the mainspring of nearly all creative endeavor. The greatest urge of man is to achieve his potentials, to contribute something of value to his fellow man. To feel that his life is worthwhile.

If you desire to increase your creativity just become insatiably curious. *Always* ask questions, particularly WHY. The tremendous amount that a child learns in his first five years could only be accomplished because of the questions he asks. Uninhibited questioning, imagination, and fantasy, develop creativity.

### *A good example is the best stimulant for creativity*

The creative spirit spreads best through personal contagion. Faraday, not having a sophisticated education, and by starting out as a boy cleaning up in Sir Humphrey Davies' laboratory, received the full impact of the great scientist's example. In his own later work Faraday didn't realize that he was subject to limitations. He was typical of all amateurs of all times and of all countries. Faraday did not know what could not be done and went right ahead and did it.

Not so long ago I visited one of the great electronic laboratories in the West. When I asked the director for some examples of what he called creativity, he mentioned one of his technicians. The director had asked several of the major glass companies for help in bonding metal and glass in the construction of a large television tube. Without exception, the glass company "experts" replied that such a bond could not be made. The director, in passing through the shop asked a technician to make such a bond for him when he had time. Shortly afterward the tube was delivered with no comment about any difficulty. The technician simply had tried a type of flux that the glass companies had not used, and had succeeded.

### *The fear of ridicule is a deadly block to creativity*

You can expect your creative efforts to be discouraged by others. There is little you can do to prevent a person who is afraid of change from opposing ideas which, if accepted, would force him to change. There are a great many people like this, and unfortunately they are often found in positions of authority and supposed leadership.

You can eliminate for yourself the far more deadly and absolutely unnecessary drag of self-discouragement. Just match up your boundless creative power against the puny efforts of those who would frustrate you by killing your creative ideas before they are full born.

While gathering ideas do not waste your time wondering whether an idea will work out or not. If you try to put it into a solution you have a chance to succeed, either as planned or in a modified manner. If you do not even try you are bound to fail. Then, too, failure depends on the point of view. Until your objective and those around you are brought together, seeming failure often results. This is the time to harmonize your objectives, and then to try again.

Any great idea is one that will greatly change men's habits or beliefs. Most people don't like to change their minds and to protect themselves very often successfully crush new ideas by laughing at them. In such ridicule they are joined by others who want to hold on to their old, comfortable beliefs. Also, it is highly important to remember that even a very good idea can be ahead of its time and if adopted could cause too great disruption. More planning is needed.

### *Too much pressure inhibits creativity*

While commitments, deadlines, quotas and other spurs to creativity are helpful, too much pressure will block creativity.

If the pressure comes from within, in some form of motivation, the results are usually good. I know one manager who has achieved remarkable results by walking up to an employee and asking, "What are you thinking about?"

After answering "nothing" a couple of times the employee begins to try to give some constructive answer. Eventually, knowing that this question will continue to be asked, the employee starts looking around him for something really creative to suggest. It is very provocative to the suggestion of more good ideas if the manager acknowledges the merit of the idea to the employee in question, but it is far more effective if the commendation is given in the presence of other employees.

No high level creative work comes from external compulsion applied to the research worker. Good work is done only when there is a deep inner compulsion on the part of the researcher himself.

There is much evidence for the statement that people will think better when not pushed too hard. Imagination tends to be cramped under excessive pressure. One of my scientist friends went into Germany soon after the capitulation of that country as part of a team looking for great new scientific discoveries that had been produced and concealed by the Germans. The pressure of the Nazi leadership not only had failed to increase the famed

German creativity but had reduced it to a level far below that of peacetime.

You just can't be creative if there is somebody standing at your elbow forcing you to produce. This is the time to be creative in finding relief from the pressure, and to establish for yourself the conditions of freedom and of relaxation that are conducive to creativity. One executive of my acquaintance would sometimes take the train on short journeys of a few hundred miles so that he could control the pressure upon him. The certainty of being able to think without distraction brought ideas.

## 2. Be Original

### *The meaning of originality*

Creativity takes originality, which means the production of novel applications of the forces and materials of nature—through new combinations of existing or newly acquired ideas.

In the year 1907 American-made cars were in very bad repute in Europe because replacement parts would seldom fit. When Henry Leland met Carl Johansson and bought a set of what are now known as "Jo Blocks" he was able to turn this unhappy condition into a success that won for Cadillac the greatly coveted Dewar trophy. This trophy was awarded by the Royal Automobile Club of London, England, for the greatest advance in automobile production. By applying his $1500 set of "Jo Blocks" to Cadillac production, Leland obtained such accuracy that he was able to drive three new Cadillacs to an English race track, to completely disassemble the cars and mix the parts up in one big pile, and then permit some English judges to remove nearly one hundred parts, replacing them with other parts from the stock of a dealer. The three cars were then re-assembled, taken out on the track, and successfully put through a gruelling 500-mile test.

Creativity involves a contribution to an art, originality as distinct from routine applications of known skills. It is relatively easy to form new combinations of old ideas that are different. It is only when these combinations are different and better, that they are classified as creative.

***Originality involves discovery***

Because creativity probes the unknown it discovers new ideas to use directly or in combination with old ideas. Discovery comes as the result of a positive discontent, a constructive dissatisfaction. In fact, one may quite truthfully say that there is no discovery when one is content, except by accident.

It was not common sense to put a man into orbit around the earth, because common sense means living in a status quo world. Creative people do not want the world as it is today, but want to make a newer, a better world.

***Characteristics of an original person***

The *Original Person,* according to Dr. Frank Barron, the Director of the Institute of Personality Assessment and Research, at the University of California in Berkeley, California, has fairly specific characteristics. The predominant attributes of the original person are that he is: intelligent, widely-informed, concerned with basic problems, clever, imaginative, socially effective, personally dominant, verbally fluent, and possessed of initiative. The original person has a philosophy of independent thinking and pursues at all costs the investigation of whatever he becomes curious about. This curiosity is insatiable. The driving spirit of inquiry can not be satiated by repression or substitution, but must be allowed to express itself if the individual himself is not to be harmed.

No one person is highly original in all areas. One may be a fluent originator of ideas, another a good methodologist. The problem of an administrator is to match up qualities in such a way as to offer all that is needed for a particular job.

A gentleman of purely "practical" education called on me to tell me of his original method of prospecting for oil. He had read that there was a certain type of bacteria, called Desulforibrio, that lived on the gases that come up from oil deep in the earth, by seepage.

Research at Scripps Institute of Oceanography had confirmed the large excess of these bacteria around oil producing areas.

My visitor claimed to have observed some condition, to which he was sensitive without instruments, that indicated to him the presence of Desulforibrio. While, of course, I was not informed of the methods he used, I was shown evidence of some success in the discovery of producing oil fields.

## 3. Avoid "Bit" Thinking

### *Thinking for survival*

Einstein, the great scientist who pointed the way for the world to blow itself up, has also pointed the way to survival. "A new kind of thinking is necessary if mankind is to survive."

What is this *new* kind of thinking? It is "Whole" thinking, morphological thinking, in contrast to the "Bit" thinking that characterizes far too much of our national thinking. "Bit" thinking is a "hang-over" from the once golden days of rugged individualism. Now, if we are to survive, either as individuals or as a nation, we must consider the total sphere in which our actions are potent.

### *Bit thinking in American education*

American educational philosophy seems to fall into two distinct and warring categories. One wants to remain "pure" by keeping aloof from existing problems in the daily lives of the people. Mathematics people say, "No, we will not talk about problems that exist in industry, because they will be different when the students graduate and face problems. It would just be a waste of time." Those of my readers who are responsible for hiring students trained under this philosophy are well familiar with the ineptitude of these students, when asked to approach and to handle new problems of any kind.

The other philosophy says never mind all this theory, just teach the students to do something so that they will be worth hiring when they get out of school.

Neither group alone can possibly be right. Institutions such as Antioch College and the University of Cincinnati have been able to do both, with outstanding success. Of course they have broken with some "pet" theories of education and have incurred powerful antagonists. But the truth, when presented, raises many questions about the normal *"bit"* thinking fostered and insisted upon by American Education.

***"Bit" thinking in the U.S. government***

I have personally visited one farming community in Minnesota where the inhabitants were paid many thousands of dollars for taking good wheat land out of production. The same people were being paid more money to help them reclaim swamp land to put into wheat land acreage which, in a few more years, "Uncle Santa-Claus" would pay more money to retire. All of this money was coming from the same federal department.

***"Bit" thinking in international relations***

The Western Powers carried on World War II through to total military victory and unconditional military surrender. During the war there apparently had been little or no thought given to post war problems, or post war strategy. The Soviets, while still in the hot war, were "thinking whole" and looking forward to post war actions. The Soviets realistically secured and satellized buffer states. The Communist group continued its "whole" thinking, and as the result have been calling the turns ever since.

I am sure that there must have been *some* intelligent persons in the group who accepted responsibility for West Berlin but who forgot to be certain that there was land passage available for us and our associates to reach Berlin. It is still an unanswered question how such "Bit" thinking could have ever been allowed to become a part of our international diplomacy.

A report from Communist China, given in *Science News Letter*, of December 10, 1960, describes in great detail their purported advances since 1950. Whether we need to discredit their claims or not may be a question. The significant aspect of the Chinese report is the very extensive emphasis that is laid on the "Total" thinking of the Communist government. This is the greatest source of their strength, which we can no longer afford to laugh off.

If American Education, and American Government, will recognize the power of "total" thinking in time, while remembering that it is not necessary to destroy individualism, as have the Communists, we can become strong enough to survive against the odds.

## 4. Use Your Imagination

### *What is imagination*

All problems are solved by imagination; the creative person has a vivid imagination. Imagination, while the power to bring images into consciousness, is also an action of the mind that *produces* a new idea, or insight. Imagination also means the ability, or process of thinking in images, to bring out of chaos order and beauty.

Imagination and intuition function together with the intellect in forming a total concept. Closure, the tendency of the mind to complete an incomplete picture, is basic in imagination. Related to closure is combination, as the essence of imagination. There seems to be little, if any, relationship between so-called intelligence and imagination. Persons, who by any conceivable standard would not be called intelligent, and others who are under the influence of drugs, dreams, or hypnosis are frequently highly imaginative. The question is not if you have imagination, but whether or not you are willing to release it.

### *There is no limit to your imagination*

It is very rarely that one sees a healthy child who is not imaginative. Yet something happens in the home, and in the schools, that causes most children to grow up to be non-creative.

The first thing to do if you want to be creative is to make an optimistic start. Dream up the biggest dream that you possibly can, in the area in which you are most anxious to make real progress. Soar off into space on your grand idea, expending every effort to realize your dream, and you probably will.

The more that you will let your imagination zoom freely the more likely you will be to experience what we call inspiration. The flash of understanding that results in a sound solution for a problem often comes while the imagination is flying off in search of something else. Trying to combine judgment with imagination is like tying five pound weights onto the feet of a high jumper. In approaching a problem, or in looking for ideas for solutions, give imagination priority, suspend judgment until it appears likely that a good solution or two may be waiting to be formed from the available ideas.

One of the best ways to release your imagination, after you have done some hard work on your problem, is to relax completely, with your feet up, and to enter into a sort of reverie. What is really going on is the numbing of the conscious mind, that normally tries to ride herd on the subconscious mind. The subconscious is thus free to move around its vast storehouse of ideas until the association or combination desired is found.

### *Be interested in everything*

The creative person has an interest in all problems that come to his attention. This interest will be developed more rapidly if you develop the habit of reacting "yes" to a new idea. This does not mean that you must, or should, accept or believe all ideas presented, but to have the attitude that the idea might be good, and something worth while can be done with it.

If you are manufacturing a product that you want to be of the very best quality possible, be especially interested in the needs of those who will eventually use your product. As you become those persons, visualize yourself using the product and react as if you had spent your money for it . . . how would you feel?

When an interest in solving a problem goes beyond awareness, it becomes active curiosity.

### *Be curious about everything*

The Creative person has a relentless curiosity. If you wish to be creative you must be curious. Curiosity involves an inquiring mind and a vivid imagination. In creative efforts one asks himself the biggest question he can think of and then tries everything he can think of to find answers.

A creative questioner is continually investigating the basic principles of his predecessors. If he does not question, he condemns himself to working to a greater and greater extent on detailed and trivial levels.

When you release your creative imagination, you will be continually hunting around you for things to improve and will then take steps to improve them.

Creative imagination is not comfortable. As an inventor expressed it to me recently, "I am plagued with curiosity about everything around me. Why is a steering wheel round? Why is it necessary for me to carry a spare tire? Why does an automobile need a three hundred horsepower engine?"

Curiosity is interest with legs. A truly curious person *has* to *do* something about any condition which has aroused his interest. Creativity involves the maximum use of imagination and resourcefulness. The creative person says, "This is a clumsy way; there must be a better way." One inventor being sufficiently annoyed at the way that fluid meters stopped the free flow of liquids, devised a meter that operated like an electric generator. The liquid served as the armature and a pair of vanes as the brushes. A strong magnetic field was electrically induced to complete the generator. The potential developed gave a very accurate indication of the amount of liquid that was flowing in the pipe.

## 5. Utilize Your Unlimited Subconscious Power

### *The nature of the subconscious*

The conscious self is narrowly limited, but the scope of the subconscious has never been determined. It probably has no limits.

Our difficulty in appreciating our creative potentials lies in our inability, *at the level of consciousness,* to catch up with our *subconscious* potentialities. The subconscious is a new frontier for most people, and something that most people are afraid to know about.

Out of the subconscious comes the ability to dream, to indulge in fantasy, to laugh, to be spontaneous, to play, to be humorous.

The subconscious mind works in some free association when

searching for a solution to a problem. The subconscious keeps working on a problem even though the individual may be unaware, consciously, of this activity. A great deal of what we are writing about is rooted in subconscious activity, of which we are not conscious.

The subconscious is by no means inferior to the conscious. The subconscious is capable of discernment. It has tact, sensitivity and the ability to make selections from tremendous stores of concepts and ideas. In fact, there seems to be little doubt that a subconscious intelligence is called for.

The experience that furnishes the material for artistic expression still is not familiar. It is a mysterious something that emerges from the remote darkness of man's mind. In poetry it is the spontaneous overflowing of very powerful feelings. The verse as written is simply a poetical arrangement of the subconscious thoughts, combined and disclosed.

### *Subconscious creativity*

"I have no idea whence this tide comes, or whence it goes. But when it begins to rise in my heart, I know that a story is hovering in the offing," is the way one writer expressed the beginnings of his writing. The material is psychically assimilated by the poet, lifted from the level of the commonplace up to that of poetic experience. The world we create is an expression of our inner wishes and thoughts.

The process of writing is not simply a subconscious memory of a vision, but is the same process that fabricated the dream.

Much fruitless effort is expended in trying to force the completion of creative work by sheer will power, instead of waiting for subconscious development. What will be best in your creative product you really do not know. If you did know beforehand the process would not be creation, but dictation. One writer said that his own method is to give no thought whatever to the form of what he is writing. "My subconscious registered their vision, my hand recorded my sensations."

As a writer becomes highly skilled he develops the ability, while writing, of being also present as a spectator and of being indifferent or impassioned as would another reader.

The subconscious is no tool for the lazy man. The work of the subconscious is fruitful only if it is both preceded and followed by periods of conscious, hard work. No intellectual power will induce a poem if the subconscious is not ready, and the conscious training of the poet must fill in what has been left out by the subconscious.

The creative aspects of life, as expressed most clearly in art, continue to baffle all attempts to formulate by logic or rational activity. His own work, when completed, is often incomprehensible to the composer, immediately after it has been completed. The writer often puts down things that he does not understand himself, feeling certain that later on they will become clear and meaningful.

Many creative persons with whom I have held extended conferences, have said that they are unaware of the thought processes which they are using, and sometimes which they have used. "When you start to paint," an artist said, "You shut your 'eyes' and work under the direction of instinct and intuition. The picture comes out of instinct, intuition, and physical action. Once the instinct and intuition get into the brush tip, the picture happens."

### *The subconscious is indispensable*

The creative is not to be found by an examination of the conscious scene—it is not there. Creativity involves both conscious and subconscious activity. Creative work arises from the depths of the subconscious. Still a great mystery is the power, that from the countless products of the subconscious, selects the ones that pass through to the conscious.

Many scientists have told me that they have never experienced a significant breakthrough, during the course of their work, without the direct aid of their subconscious, after the failure of their conscious efforts. An increased facility in making use of the subconscious makes one able to play with ideas and, as it were, to sail right off into the blue, free from the limitations of common sense. It has been found, too, that the existence of some irritation often inspires the actual take off.

Creativity, in its essence, is the investigation of the unknown. To many, creativity is a fearsome thing suggesting change, destruction, unemployment, and lack of security. How to help you make this leap into the dark, out of which is born new hypotheses is one of the aims of this book.

The formulation of hypotheses, from the mass of data that one has accumulated, is largely the product of the subconscious. An individual who has difficulty in the formation of hypotheses will be helped greatly as he learns to eliminate those forces that are inhibiting the work of his subconscious.

### *For "whole" thinking use both the conscious and subconscious*

The creative person has achieved some measure of harmony between the operations of his conscious and subconscious. A strong tendency does exist for the conscious to limit the activities of the subconscious. The strong urge of the subconscious to propose new solutions is often the cause of much uneasiness on the part of the conscious.

One of the most far-reaching insights of Freud was the realization that processes in the brain of which we were quite unaware may dominate much conscious activity. While the individual may be consciously afraid of fantasy, his subconscious is not so inhibited.

One of the unfortunate effects of accepting Freud too enthusiastically is that many have come to regard their inner selves as dangerous. As the result, many have endeavored to wall off the offered contributions of the subconscious, the greatest source of power available to them.

Because the creation of a poem involves re-ordering of subconscious concepts, it can not be forced and developed wholly by conscious effort. The writing of a poem is a matter of making moment-by-moment selections from the unlimited possibilities proposed by the subconscious. The alternate conscious and subconscious digestion has been likened to the rumination of a cow.

### *Listening to the subconscious*

First of all respect *your* hunches. This does not mean to rush off and put in effect immediately every idea that comes to your mind. It does mean to respect each hunch, at least to the extent of writing it down for future consideration. Einstein carried one hunch for many years without being able to substantiate it. It finally led to the general theory of relativity. All scientists and inventors I have queried give much credit to their hunches.

The poet's part in the writing of a poem is to follow the dictation of something within himself. "I do not hear a voice, but I do hear the words pronounced in a toneless manner. The words seem to be pronounced within my head with nobody speaking."

### *Factors of the subconscious*

Among the subconscious drives is the one called motivation. Where *incentive* is the product of the environment, *motivation* originates and impels from within. Due to its emotional response, motivation is stimulated by excitement of many kinds. Certainly the effects of an enthusiastic cheering section has been the cause of many sports victories. The inner aroused excitement that comes with a sense of progressing creativity is also a factor in creative achievement.

The power from a drawn bow becomes available only when the tension is relaxed. So also in creative efforts, the solution of a problem usually comes after an interval of relaxed interest. The achievement seems almost to be a reward, as the result of freedom given the subconscious mind.

Patience during the period of relaxed incubation, gives the ideas that have been loosened up a chance to swoosh around in the subconscious, producing new combinations as the result of their collisions.

The end product of the incubation process, intuition, comes when the image has been completed and submitted to the conscious mind. Intuition is the bond between the unknown that we feel and the unknown which we seek.

The creative person has a very strong sense of intuition, and in addition a willingness to follow it. In the solving of problems intuition involves a vivid imagination as well as an alert nature.

At the peak of a creative experience when thoughts and powers are integrated and coordinated it is said that insight has been had. The process leading up to and following the moment of insight is inspiration.

Creative design requires an inspired approach more than the organized approach. Persons with this attribute are considered to be rare treasures in any organization.

The moment of insight can be expected more often in dispersed attention than in concentrated attention, following long periods of hard work. Inspiration is not a sudden flash but is a clearly felt impulse toward a goal, which the person is striving to reach. In poetry, inspiration is both the beginning of a poem and also its final goal. Inspiration, then, is the impulse which sets creation in motion and the energy which keeps it going. The moment of insight which characterizes creative or inventive thinking is followed, normally, by explicit, deductive thinking during the testing of the new idea. Logic comes after the moment of insight. Things fall into place after you have the inspiration. Previous to this there is a set of unrelated elements.

## 6. Be Open-Minded

***Creativity is open-mindedness***

Open-mindedness is so vital to creative achievement that it is necessary to reject some ideas. This seems like a very contradictory statement but it is very true.

When Frederic N. Schwartz, the president of Bristol-Myers pharmaceutical company, was asked to define his job, he said, "It is to try to keep closed minds open."

Once you have accepted the idea that any one procedure is the only way that should be employed in the solving of a problem, then any ideas that do not fit into the pattern suggested are automatically sidetracked, and perhaps permanently lost.

We are *not* suggesting that any idea that comes your way should be accepted as truth, and immediately acted upon. What we are stressing is the absolutely essential habit of *receiving* and parking all ideas as offered, as many and as divergent as they come. Make no immediate evaluation.

This free reception of ideas is basic to open-mindedness upon which the highest level of creative achievement rests. It is impossible to be at once selective in the acceptance of ideas and free from prejudice.

All this is not to say that an attitude of healthy skepticism is not to be preferred to the complacent acceptance of anything expressed in your presence. But skepticism does not mean rejection, it does mean that the idea under question will be "taken in out of the rain," just in case you are mistaken in your opinion. This kind of an idea may be greatly changed in significance after all available ideas have been synthesized and their associated meanings discovered. For an analogy, if you were walking up a mountain any attempt by a companion to place a steel nut in your shoe would be opposed vigorously. A steel nut has no place at all in this picture. But on the other hand, if your planned activity was to coast down hill on a wagon and you noted that a rear wheel was about to fall off, then the nut would have an indispensable place in your life.

If you will think about the reception by your senior on the job of some of your ideas, you will recognize that it was not your ideas that had been rejected so much as failure to see the need of them. The acceptance of a new idea often introduces many changes, changes mean extra work and some danger.

### *Open-mindedness to new ideas*

If one yields too often to his natural tendency to reject ideas, he is forced to attempt to solve problems by the use of earlier solutions only. The tendency to solve problems by adding elements to old solutions very often results in clumsy solutions. The modifications of familiar solutions, in place of occasionally going back to the basic fundamentals of the problem, is one of the political blunders the American Foreign Office has been making that has kept us on the defensive for so long. Our opponents, even though they have the wrong objectives, owe much of their strength to their open-mindedness to ideas that differ from their own.

The acceptance of new ideas, in the sense of receiving them for later evaluation, is the very best way for you to be offered a great quantity of ideas, among which may be the new one of great power for which you are seeking.

### *Open-mindedness to impulses*

The creative person welcomes his *creative* impulses because he has discovered that great achievements often come when he does. Once again, here is suggested an action that can also be harmful. How is one to choose which impulse to follow?

There is no simple, hard and fast rule. A guiding philosophy that many have found dependable is to yield at once if nobody will be harmed by the result of their action, or if the consequences may be readily corrected if they prove undesirable.

Impulses usually float up from the depths of your unconscious and often are directing forces to a great good not appreciated by the conscious. A period of brief contemplation also helps.

### *Open-mindedness to change*

Far too often, traditional methods lead to the attempted use of yesterday's solutions to today's problems. Because the improvement in airplane compasses had done wonders in enabling over-ocean flights to conclude successfully on a tiny island at a great distance from other land, the trouble experienced by jet pilots in getting airborne while moving in a given direction suggested increasing the accuracy of the compass.

Persistent inquiry on the part of investigators finally brought out the basic fact that the pilot's difficulty was that of staying on the runway until airborne, knowing the compass heading in which the plane was moving was of itself of little importance. When this was realized there came a willingness on the part of both pilots and manufacturers to change their thinking from the development of a better directional gyro to the design of some method of keeping the airplane on the runway until it had become airborne.

### *Growth depends on open-mindedness*

There is nothing that a person craves more than the consciousness that he is growing. Riches, fame, authority, all prove to be hollow achievements unless, during the period of their acquisition, you are conscious of a growth in personality. The expression of your personality and creative achievement are synonymous with growth. Growth, in turn, depends for maximum attainment upon the maintenance of the attitude of open-mindedness.

The creative person has broad interests and is constantly growing. Two of the members of the Pacific Coast Football Conference board of governors were Nobel Laureate Glen Seaborg, then the Chancellor of the University of California Berkeley Campus, and Dr. Joseph Kaplan, the U.S. Chairman of the I.G.Y.

### *Open-mindedness to truth*

When truth is accepted as creation within human experience, then the detachment of the individual constitutes objectivity. The creative person can at the same time give himself intensely to an experience, and keep an eye on his emergent behavior. Simultaneous involvement and detachment will help a writer avoid falling in love with some highly artistic phrase, that really does not belong to the statement being developed.

There is probably nothing that is so much resisted as truth. This is the philosophy expressed by Rabelais, the judge, when he said, "My mind is made up. Don't confuse me with the truth." When an honest person sees the truth in a situation, he is under an irresistable obligation to so order his conduct as to be in harmony with the truth.

Truth usually means change. Change requires courage to face the unknown. Creativity requires courage to face the opposition it arouses to the changes that will be brought about. But, as creativity is growth, if we would grow then we must be open-minded to truth—from wherever it comes.

### *Open-mindedness to experience*

Experience provides much of the raw material for creativity and meaning for the end results. The significance of a new idea lies in its possible relationships with existing ideas. An appreciation of improvement can be had only with a less desirable standard of comparison.

A creative person is open to experience both in his external environment and to changes within himself. The two are more one totality than two entities, for the individual is constantly interacting with his environment.

Experience is continually being added, both environmentally and subconsciously. It is for this reason that highly creative people invariably have several projects under way at the same time. Each project is sending out feelers to the environment and into the subconscious and replies in the form of ideas are being attracted. Therefore the more projects that are under way the more chances of an oncoming idea opening the way for progress.

### *Open-mindedness to people*

While there is much conjecture and very little agreement concerning the source of non-sensory ideas—those that seem to well up from the subconscious—it is quite obvious that most of our ideas come from people.

It would seem, therefore, that it would be profitable to treat people in such a way as to stimulate the flow of people ideas. There is nothing magic about the attitude that results in the free offer of ideas. What is required is the reception of all ideas offered and treating them with appreciation and respect. Before attempting to evaluate the idea from your own point of view try to understand the viewpoint of the giver of the idea. It may be that your own viewpoint needs to be modified, at least to the extent that the other person's view has truth in it. There is never any difficulty in synthesizing truths when they are seen by all persons who are attempting to work harmoniously together for the greatest good of all concerned.

## 7. Reduce Mental Tension

### *You can be free from mental tension*

The basic principle underlying the reduction of mental stress is to recognize the causes and then to refuse to act in such a way as to result in inner tension.

"One who would be a creative genius," said Dr. Aaron Wexler, head of the Westinghouse Research Laboratories in Pittsburgh, "must have a lack of concern in being wrong, must have the ability to shrug off wrong guesses."

As a job nears completion, or a problem approaches solution, the tension builds up. Delays or objections that would cause little reaction earlier increase in their frustrating effect. It is at this point that the practice of seeing the total picture directs the elements of a solution into their proper positions. Keeping the whole pattern in mind relieves one from the fear that one of the essential elements has been forgotten.

While the vision of perfection is useful to give direction to your activities, the *demanding* of self or others that perfection be *reached* must be avoided, if destructive tensions are to be absent. Adverse effects of thinking under pressure can best be avoided by the use of foresight. If it is known that a certain report must be ready by a given date, for example, there is nothing to prevent you from having all material ready just as soon as you possibly can.

There are many cycles in both men and women. The creative cycle as well as the moods that make for creativity have ups and downs. The period of these cycles can be determined by the keeping of a diary. While one often can produce when the creativity curve is in a depression, the amount of energy required and the greatly increased danger of failure justifies a delay.

Patience is a great help in maintaining freedom from mental tension. Successful story writers report that their articles will sometimes simmer for years before they can be written. When a good idea comes to you that does not seem to fit, be sure to write it down for it may be very slow in returning. It is highly frustrating at a later date to realize that you once had the missing key to some situation but cannot now remember it.

### *Environmental causes of mental tension*

The social environment through both conscious and subconscious affects the individual. Many have lost freedom to believe in themselves, in their associates, and in life, because they have become so impressed with the power of their environment over them. Pioneers with a minimum of equipment settled in undeveloped areas and lived successfully. In a tougher environment, and with fewer aids, the pioneer lived with greater confidence. The pioneer's climate demanded creativity; ours often inhibits it.

Today the pressure is for conformity. The environment demands little in the way of imaginative exercise. You must demand it for yourself. Most people in modern society do only what others have done before them. If they have original ideas they fail to develop them. The craving of a young man to test his daring, is denied the youth of today—except when a war comes along—and then the eighteen-year-old grows up overnight.

I asked one of this country's most creative men if his son had followed in his creative footsteps. His reply was that his son had never been hungry, and had never demonstrated the characteristics that had controlled him, the father.

The freedom to create has moved from on the job to off the job. Some try to be creative by buying gadgets, by patronizing spectator sports, by undertaking do-it-yourself projects around the house. Trade unions and our taxing "methods," regardless of all inherent benefits, are dedicated to the ideal of bringing all individuals to a common level, thereby destroying initiative.

As the standards of living progressively rise there is more and more the tendency to be satisfied, to be comfortable.

Much mental tension is aroused by attempting to forcibly overthrow these environmental causes, many of which are beyond your ability to change. What can always be done successfully is to become active in several other areas in which you do have control over your activities. If your salary job is the production of stock machine pieces, for which you are well paid, the monotony of your work can be so diluted by your creative achievements in writing, painting, toy repair for the children of the neighborhood, etc., as to be of minimum concern.

### *Emotional causes of mental tension*

Many of the problems associated with creativity are in the forms of emotional blocks within one's self. These must be solved first before significant creative achievement can be expected.

One serious block to creativity fostered by our culture is the national fear of failure. Young and old are taught to fear and to avoid failure and to worship success.

In addition to the fear of making a mistake—or arising from it—is the fear of making a fool of one's self. Even the certain knowledge of the correctness of one's position does not seem to alleviate this fear on many occasions. From these fears comes a pathological desire for security, for conformity. High school graduates seeking employment are more concerned with job security than with job opportunity.

One morning, when I was a young man working for a public utility corporation, I was quite surprised at the sharpness with which my usually goodnatured Irish boss snapped back at me when I made a request. Almost immediately, however, he explained everything by saying, "Ah, forget it, I have just come from a deaf and dumb breakfast." As A. H. Maslow so aptly expresses it, "There was a projection to the outside of an inner civil war."

While waiting for my appointment with the manager of a large J. C. Penney store, I was very favorably impressed with the attitude displayed by the employees to each other, as they entered and left the head offices. I later commented upon this to the manager who explained, "We don't allow hate anywhere in this store."

### *Psychological causes of mental tension*

Creative thinking is healthy thinking—total thinking. The fully evolved person is available to himself on both conscious and subconscious levels simultaneously. As things stand for most people the two are walled off from each other. The process of getting the conscious and the subconscious working together is largely one of faith, by consciously giving problems and ideas to the subconscious and expecting a helpful reply. This you will always receive as soon, perhaps even before, as you confidently expect assistance.

A strong desire to create is essential in the creative process.

The desire is actually always present and when your self-imposed blocks are removed you will be creative in your achievements.

It is well to remember that the creative flow in individuals is not going to be continuous; it will always be pulsating. As mentioned earlier, we do not yet know the cycles or how to control their appearances. It is certain, however, that upon completion of a creative activity there is a low level of energy which should be increased by rest, or change of activity.

Some people are so burdened by their inhibitions, by an extensive knowledge of all the reasons why whatever is attempted can not succeed, that the mere suggestion of an untried idea is immediately rejected.

The labeling of things as obvious, and the refusal of seeing them as *new* or in a *new* relationship, has the tendency to limit flexibility and originality of thinking. This is another form of prejudice that influences our capacity to use our minds to the maximum.

# 5

## HOW TO BE CREATIVE

### *Creative action after creative thinking*

Once we are thinking creatively our next action is to take steps toward the achievement of our goals. We need initiative in order to overcome our inertia. We must get started or we will never achieve anything.

Sensitivity to conditions around us is one of the prime essentials for creativity, and for getting us moving. We should be sensitive to needs to be met, opportunities to be seized, and problems to be solved.

In order to be creative we must be flexible to any change in our environment if we are to be sensitive to real problems in need of solving.

If we are able to make good decisions we must have acquired many things to choose from. We must resist pressures to be satisfied with "bit" thinking, based on insufficient knowledge.

### *The greatest creative force*

The recognition of, and a deep respect for, your *need* to be creative—to grow—is by all odds the greatest influence for creative achievement. This growth need is never satisfied, even temporarily, as is a deficit need, such as hunger. Even on relatively low levels, an achievement made possible by growth in some ability stimulates efforts to accomplish something a little more difficult. A baseball pitcher, whose mastery of a certain pitch has enabled him for the first time to win sixteen ball games in a season, now sees the magic of being a twenty-game winner within his grasp.

## 1. Develop Initiative

### *"Dare to have a purpose"*

Initiative is not something that you either have or do not have. Initiative is a potential that exists in every one of us. It is something like the possible energy stored up in a mountain lake. When a connection is made, between our initiative and a subject for action, the power of our latent initiative is expressed.

An objective so clear as to be unmistakable and so desirable that one is not inclined to count the cost in its attainment sparks initiative, the beginning of creative achievement. Unrealistic goals, whose attainment will be long delayed, will serve to extinguish creative sparks. This does not mean that we are not to establish a high level, long time objective toward which we move but never reach, but simply that along the projected pathway there shall be markers, or mile-posts, so that we can feel our progress.

### *Concentrate on a problem*

You will never get what you want until you know what it is.

We do best what we are happiest in doing, what we really want to do. In order to solve a problem you must want, must desire to solve it. There is nothing that will bring to life dormant initiative more than the recognition and an understanding of a problem that needs to be solved. If you are one of the many who gets things done when you really get going, but who have trouble making a start, look around you for a problem that interests you.

Creative motivation comes from the recognition of a problem, a feeling of responsibility, and a sufficient understanding of the surrounding medium to bring it to bear on the problem. There is a great deal of personal satisfaction in getting at the roots of a problem you are trying to solve.

### *How to find problems*

You will find all the problems that you can possibly want if you will just be open-minded. Be open-minded to ideas, to the unknown, to growth, and to the emergence of the new from the old. Steam locomotives have left American railroads because the emergence of the new, the diesel engine, was seen by railroad management. This recognition wasn't pleasant, because it meant the discarding of a very faithful servant that had much to do with the growth of our great country.

The creative person seeks to extend his experiencing by holding himself open for ever broadening inclusions, by a taste for adventure and by seeking to understand what is going on within and around himself.

### *How to release your initiative*

The first step in the release of your initiative is to develop an overwhelming interest in some problem and then to be discontented with whatever you find by way of actual or proposed solutions. An inventor said to me, "I am constantly dissatisfied with things as they are. I am interested in the abolition of waste and complication. I don't assume that anything is *really* good." To have discontent does not mean complaining, it means a *constructive discontent,* believing that "there *must* be a better way."

Following an interest in whatever exists around you comes a curiosity about how things work and why they are done as they are. Then comes an endless questioning involving what about, what if, what else, etc. The right questions asked in the right way, comprise the best possible preparation for solving a problem.

While irritation is probably the first step in the creative process, I suppose that the real essence of creativity is to *do something* about it when you are irritated. Recognition of a situation that should be improved and subsequent action mark the real beginning of initiative. An inventor friend of mine remarked, "When I see something that *can* be improved, I ask myself why not DO something about it? There is usually no good reason why I should not follow my own suggestion."

### *Some characteristics of initiative*

A vigorous courage, that will make likely independence of thought and action, is a characteristic seldom absent in the personality demonstrating initiative. The creative person insists on controlling, to a large degree, his own work schedule and expresses a willingness to stick with baffling problems for as long a period as is useful. The role of scientists and inventors is full of people who quit one school because they had different ideas as to what they should study than did the teachers. Roentgen, the discoverer of X-rays, and Edison, the great inventor, are but two of many who might be named.

Knowledge can be found in all persons; enthusiasm, however, is a great rarity. A creative person has basic enthusiasm for a problem facing him. Ideas without drive are cheap and plentiful. The creative person not only has great emotional, mental, and physical drive, but also the willingness to channel this ability in useful directions.

A strong spirit of adventure, a great craving to get out to the very edges of conscious realization, to reach beyond conformity, to feel a way into the unknown—all these are inherent in initiative. Adventure, creativity, initiative, all require much energy. Adventurous researchers such as E. O. Lawrence, the inventor of the cyclotron, were known for their exceptional drive and energy, physical and emotional as well as mental.

Frederich Nietzsche said, "When my creative energy flowed most freely, my muscular activity was always greatest." In other words, when you don't know what else to do to activate your initiative, go for a vigorous walk, perhaps even mow the lawn.

## 2. Develop Total Sensitivity

### *Sensitivity stimulates creativity*

John Dewey said that science begins not with facts, nor theories, nor hypotheses—but with a problematic situation. A problematic situation is one that has something in it that disturbs you. Sensitivity, then, is the ability to recognize problems, something needing to be improved.

It was a sensitive person who, after trying to open a door with both hands full and dropping part of his load asked, "Why don't they do something about this?" and then developed the electronic door opener.

Physicist C. T. R. Wilson had been wandering over the hills of his native Scotland while seeking some way to measure the charge on an electron. On seeing the clouds form on the hills as the moist air blew over them he exclaimed, "I can do this in the laboratory—put charges on the cloud and measure the charge."

People who are creative do not only see what actually exists, but what *could*.

### *How to increase your sensitivity*

Safecrackers sandpaper the ends of their fingers until the skin is so thin that the blood nearly comes through. The fingers are then sensitive enough so that the movements of the internal parts of the lock may be felt.

Intellectual sensitivity is very closely tied up with questioning. A sensitive person asks more questions than the usual person, but any person can become much more sensitive by asking a lot of questions. Sensitivity is not something that you have to go out looking for. Everybody has it, waiting to be developed. Each question that you ask brings out some characteristic that you had not seen clearly before, and develops your sensitivity just a little bit further.

### *What should you ask questions about?*

First of all do not be concerned at the response to your question. Many times somebody will attempt to ridicule your questions, either because he does not understand the significance of your question, or because he clearly does understand and a frank answer will require some change on his part.

While there are, of course, many things about which questions may be asked, those that seem to be most closely related to sensitivity are: (a) Problems in connection with common objects, (b) Improvements in implements or appliances, (c) Improvements in social institutions, (d) Variations from the normal in situations. Let us take up examples of these in detail.

### *Problems in connection with common objects*

Seeing that a gear is not functioning properly. Being aware that there is need for changes in the design of nearly every tool, device, or appliance in daily use. Seeing the defects or deficiencies in things as they exist.

It is highly stimulating to write down problems that *might* arise, as for example if a swimming pool is built in your back yard.

### *Possible improvements in common devices*

What is wrong with such common everyday devices as the telephone, the typewriter, the refrigerator?

A good way to ask a lot of questions is to watch the operation and care of the appliances and devices in your own home. Ask *what* is it supposed to do? How *well* it is doing its job? Why is its function as it is? How might the job be done better?

After asking why don't they develop a way to overcome this or that shortcoming, then suggest a couple of ways of your own. Heinrich Diesel was desperately trying to ignite the fuel in his engine without using sparkplugs. Having no success he decided to forget his troubles for a while and enjoy a good German cigar. He bit off the end of his cigar, pushed it into his face, then took out his cigar lighter, *shoved the plunger* causing the lighter fuel to be ignited, and his smoke began. At this instant he also saw how to ignite his engine fuel without sparkplugs.

### *Seeing deficiencies in plans or actions*

Take a look around you and see what kinds of plans are affecting your life. Are you satisfied with the sales tax, the income tax, your property tax? What about the grading plan under which you were evaluated while in school, or the one now in use in the school or college of your children?

Look for things that are odd, rare, unusual, apparently inconsistent—such as *yelling* at a child to be *quiet*.

Manufacturers of well-known products, blissfully content with their designs, may suddenly awake to find themselves bankrupt, or in a minor competitive position unless they are sensitive to changes in demand or on the part of their competitors.

The creative person has a greater sensitivity to "gaps" in his environment—that is, to great changes that will result when some relatively minor change has taken place. For example, when certain downtown streets were made one-way to relieve traffic, a number of businesses on the left side of the street that had been successful for many years had to close their doors. The tremendous extension of credit buying through the use of credit cards has caused many changes in our way of living.

### *Improvements in social institutions*

Suggest two or more improvements for social institutions such as marriage, religion, education, government and sports.

How do you think that medical institutions could be bettered?

Are you satisfied with the stores you patronize?

### *Variations from the normal in situations*

In a certain J. C. Penney store I was visiting I noticed a most unusual air of happiness and good feeling. This was so pronounced that I mentioned it to the store manager, remarking that I did not believe that such a condition was purely an accident.

The manager said, "Anything wrong in this store jumps out and calls for attention as it is seen against the background of my extensive experience in stores. I sense that there is some problem in a department by being sensitive to variations from normal reactions—a few clouds noticeable in a usually sunny disposition."

## 3. Develop Total Flexibility

### *The need for flexibility*

An increase in flexibility reduces the danger of prejudice in problem solving. A prejudiced view is sometimes of such long standing as to seem quite reasonable. We get our basic ideas about what makes up the cultural context of life as we are growing up. At middle age we often still act on premises which we may have acquired during high school years.

Many assumptions are made in engineering analysis. Each one must be checked as it is used in a new situation. Research directors often find themselves confronted with changing aims as a project develops.

There must be flexibility in design, a series of compromises. We are perfectly capable of developing jet engines that will put a satellite in orbit around the sun; and at the same time, of seeing human affairs around us through frames of reference appropriate to the horse and buggy days.

There is need for unconscious flexibility. Accident prone people are those having an unconscious mind-set that is not sensitive to the dangers inherent in a situation.

A creative technic is any device that enables one to break free from the restrictions of traditional thinking.

### *The nature of flexibility*

Flexibility means the having of many tricks in your bag plus confidence in your ability to use them and the willingness to try them out. The ability to adapt to conditions that are beyond proven experience is a prime attribute of flexibility.

Flexibility involves being able to see your problem as a system, within a system, within a still larger system.

The research directed by Dr. J. P. Guilford, in the department of psychology at the University of Southern California, has identified two distinct types of mental flexibility. The first type is called spontaneous flexibility. This means the ability to produce dissimilar ideas in a relatively unorganized situation. For example, if the junction of two roads begins to have traffic pile-ups, one solution might be to put in signals. Another, to lift one road over the other. Still another solution might be to stagger the quitting times of factories in the vicinity.

The General Electric Company, A. C. Spark Plugs, Radio Corporation of America, and many other firms, place very high among the objectives of their personnel training programs an increase in the willingness of employees to present diverse viewpoints.

The second type of flexibility found by Dr. Guilford is called Adaptive Flexibility. This means the recognition of changing conditions, and the ability to change a pattern of action to meet new requirements imposed by those changes. When the greatly increased runway speed of jet planes made visual guidance an impossibility, and compasses also proved to be too inaccurate to keep planes on the runway, a fundamentally new means of automatic guidance by electronic boundary sensing was developed.

### *Functional fixation—stubborn thinking*

Functional fixation is getting into such a rut that you tend to think of no other function or application for a device. Creative technics pull one away from functional fixation, and thinking in the same old ruts.

The new is threatening for the rigid person, but nothing new can happen to him if he can order it as part of past experience. If he can freeze the world of flux, and make believe that nothing is changing, he feels secure.

The dangers that the rigid person is really fighting are *dangers within himself*. However, anything in his external world that reminds him of the dangers within himself is fought whenever he sees them. It is a desperate effort at control. A good deal of his energy is taken up with it, so he is very apt to get tired simply controlling himself.

If the rigid person can proceed into the future on the basis of tried and trusted laws, rules and habits which have worked well in the past, he then feels safe and free from anxiety.

Many people offer great resistance to the consideration of a concept that does not lend itself to study by the *usual* scientific or educational procedures. Most executives have a tendency to resist any change. They have confidence in what is *now* being done, because it has served them well—why change?

Often there is found a tendency toward elaboration of themes, rather than a change of theme—a thorough restructuring of a problem.

***Some exercises to develop your mental flexibility***

Because there are elements in common for both types of flexibility we have not attempted to distinguish between them in the exercises suggested. Activities of the general type suggested were used in the positive identification of the intellectual factor of mental flexibility as a discrete characteristic of the creative person. Therefore we can be certain that giving one's self exercises in similar activities will develop flexibility.

*Exercise* 1: List other uses for a familiar object: an inner tube used as a life belt, as a gasoline storage tank, as an emergency car jack, as a pontoon to raise a sunken motor boat.

*Exercise* 2: Combining two or more common objects so as to make an entirely new one: From a rubber band and a ruler make a sling shot, paper holder, book mark, water level indicator, guide or stop for marking and cutting.

*Exercise* 3: List all the impossibilities that you can think of: picking up a glob of mercury with greasy fingers, tying up an elephant with rubber bands, teaching a frog to pilot a jet plane.

*Exercise* 4: Place a specified number of checkers on a checkerboard so that no two are in the same row, column or diagonal.

*Exercise* 5: List as many examples as you can of such things as metal objects: iron nail, brass candlestick, silver spoon, gold ring, etc.

*Exercise* 6: Find human faces hidden in a series of pictures.

*Exercise* 7: Identify which one of several basic figures is to be found in a series of complex geometric figures.

*Exercise* 8: Combine or eliminate matches to form certain designs or structures. Six matches to form four equilateral triangles, etc.

*Exercise* 9: List as many consequences as possible if a certain situation were to exist. All taxes are eliminated: no public schools, no public libraries, no wars, no politicians, etc.

*Exercise* 10: Solve problems requiring insight rather than computation or unusual knowledge: A hunter went out to hunt for a bear. He hiked two miles north from his camp, then two miles east where he killed the bear. He then dragged the bear two miles back home. What was the color of the bear? (White, at the South Pole.)

## 4. Develop Verbal Fluency

***The importance of verbal fluency***

Verbal fluency is the heart of communication, which is the essence of both education and problem solving upon which our very existence depends.

A creative process is not complete until its product has been communicated to some other person, and their feedback received by the creator. Verbal communication is something like the paper carton in which you carry home a quart of milk.

The development of verbal fluency is also related to initiative, sensitivity, flexibility, and originality. While, for convenience, we have treated these five factors of creativity as if they were distinct from one another, actually they are parts of a common structure and react mutually.

A nationwide study directed by the writer, in association with Doctors J. P. Guilford, and P. R. Merrifield, has indicated that verbal fluency plays a significant role in the creative process. Other studies have also shown that an increase in the quality of ideas produced is to be expected as the total quantity of ideas increases.

Verbal fluency is highly essential in the conscious expression of the results of mental processes, many of which take place in the subconscious.

Verbal fluency is the most directly visualized of the basic factors of creativity. It is a very good factor on which to seek improvement, because there are so many opportunities offered each day.

A conscious effort to increase verbal fluency will at the same time improve your human relationships. Because you will be better able to send and to receive communications, upon which good human relationships rest. Practice in repeating what someone has told you will develop an assurance of understanding what that person has really meant to say.

### *The nature of verbal fluency*

While there have been many excellent studies on the nature of verbal fluency, probably the most dependable and useful was made by Dr. J. P. Guilford and Dr. P. R. Christensen at the University of Southern California.

The Guilford-Christensen study has established beyond question that the factor of verbal fluency includes at least four specific related abilities.

*Ability* 1: Word Fluency

The ability to produce words that satisfy specified structural requirements. That is, words that rhyme, that end with certain suffixes, that contain specified letters, etc.

*Ability* 2: Ideational Fluency

The ability, under free conditions, to produce ideas on demand. To make a list of materials that have specified characteristics, such as, solid, liquid, gaseous, sweet, sour, electrically conductive. Brainstorming and morphology are outstanding examples used to get ideas in quantity.

*Ability* 3: Associational Fluency

The ability to produce attributes to fit a defined or specified meaning, such as writing new headlines for news articles, writing synonyms, antonyms, etc.

*Ability* 4: Expressional Fluency

The ability to produce continued discourse, such as to state the attributes two objects have in common, as a river and life; combinations of words with the first two letters given; to make sentences containing given words.

### *Exercises to develop your verbal fluency*

The objective of a football player during training is to develop his body so as to permit him to play his particular part well, and to avoid injury. He is not particularly concerned about the details of the benefits of each exercise. He has found from experience that the total effect of all the exercises has made him an All-American, and got him through an entire season without serious injury.

With an analogous thought in mind, the exercises suggested for developing your verbal fluency are not segregated by abilities. For each of the exercises allow a total of five minutes for writing down as many responses as you can.

*Exercise* 1: Write words *rhyming* with a given word: Crutch, hutch, much, such.

*Exercise* 2: Write words with specified endings: -ery, -ated, -ter, -ting, etc.

*Exercise* 3: Write words containing two or more specified letters, such as: r——l, b——g, s——e, etc.

*Exercise* 4: Produce a word that is synonymous with two given words: Money JACK President.

*Exercise* 5: Write two-word phrases, the first letter of each word given being: s—— m—— S*ave* M*oney,* S*hoot* M*ink.*

*Exercise* 6: Write words that rhyme with a certain word: BOOT, shoot, root, moot, coot, etc.

*Exercise* 7: Write alternate headlines for the main articles in your newspaper.

*Exercise* 8: Write two antonyms, or opposites, for a given word: WEAK—forceful, strong.

*Exercise* 9: Write as many synonyms as possible for a given word, as: EVIL—bad, harmful, wrong, injurious.

*Exercise* 10: Write as many uses as possible for common articles: NAIL—to hold boards together, to hang your hat, to keep out intruders, to fasten ripped trousers.

*Exercise* 11: Write four-word sentences, the first letter of each word being given: A B C D—*A*lways *B*e *C*areful *D*riving.

*Exercise* 12: Write as many other titles as possible for cartoons or situation pictures.

*Exercise* 13: Write completions to short sentences, as: The ocean is ———— blue, a source of food, contains minerals.

*Exercise* 14: Write as many *interpretations* of similes as possible. Example: *A smiling countenance is like the sun,* it lights up the room, it is reflected from others, it helps people grow.

## 5. Respect Your Need to be Creative

### *It is natural to be creative*

All persons can become more creative if they will. The mainspring of creativity is man's tendencies to become his potential.

The most mature human beings are also childlike—they can have the most fun! They can play with children, and be close to them. "Self-actualizing creativeness," to use the phrases of Dr. A. H. Maslow of Brandeis University, is like the creativeness of happy and secure children. It has the spontaneity, ease, innocence and freedom from stereotypes that characterizes the free play of children.

The greatest creative force you can have is an appreciation of, and a respect for, your *need* to be creative—to grow. Most of us have tried at some time or other to invent something. As will be described in the following section, this can be done systematically, until you can become a genius.

### *Creative achievement is your greatest need*

The mainspring of creativity seems to be the same tendency seen in the curative force of psychotherapy—man's tendency to become his potentialities. It is this tendency, as the person endeavors to be himself in forming new relationships to his environment, which is the primary motivation for creativity.

The secret of creation lies not so much in the materials or the medium, as the way in which the "artist" is able to feel the significance of his experiences. A young student of mine was so overwhelmed with the difficulties of child polio patients that he invented a spoon by which for the first time they could feed themselves. In describing his feelings as he watched a seven-year-old lift up her first spoonful independently he could only say, "I wept." Reacting to situations and needs of this type, inventors can count on receiving the ideas they need.

The creative person seeks to focus his experiences through realizing his potentials. This is demonstrated by his willingness to be different in things that make a difference, and in moving onward toward his own fulfillment even when it runs counter to the expectations and beliefs of others.

"I have an overpowering urge to design," an inventor once told me, "so much so that I once spent so much time on improving a loom that my main job was neglected—and the whole department was fired." This demonstrates what can happen when the "Esteem-Power" need of a man becomes out of balance. It is natural for one to desire the esteem of his fellows, which is sought sometimes by service, and sometimes by the usurping of power.

The work of a creative person may or may not be utilitarian in its aim. Neither in art nor in science is the use always anticipated. It is possible to be productive without being practical. The leading research laboratories of this country have discovered, that to keep up scientific interest in solving "company" problems, that those capable of finding solutions must be allowed scientific excursions down attractive side roads, with no obligation to bring back specific, directly applicable results. If this truth were appreciated more fully by administrators the scientific achievements of their staffs would be materially increased.

### *To live is to be creative, to grow*

To be creative does not of necessity mean to write a poem, to paint a picture, or to make an invention, but it *always* means *to solve a problem.*

To Grow means to be Creative. To be creative means to Solve Problems. Therefore, to grow means that you must solve problems.

In solving problems, when you find that you are blocked, it means that you are asking the wrong questions.

When a tree, an organization, or a person stops growing, stops living creatively, it begins dying. In this truth lies the great urge for creative expression that dominates the human personality. You will always get your greatest satisfaction from your own *creating*. A simple flower bed prepared and developed by one's own hands, far exceeds in satisfaction that derived from an elegant professional creation.

Any kind of an organism—vegetable, animal, or human—operates as a dynamic whole. Undue mental pressure affects the stomach, and in order for the stomach to recover, the mental pressure must be removed. I will, at this point nobly resist going into personal details, but I learned my lesson.

There is here a great positive implication for all who would be creative. When faced by a solid block, that does not yield no matter what you do, stop—rest—relax. Let the matter drop entirely no matter what pressures are upon you to come up with an immediate solution. Pick up an earlier problem that has been resting and you will always find that you can now make some progress. This new release of creative energy lifts you to a higher level. When you return to the original problem, you will go forward, even though but a short while ago you were absolutely blocked.

As you are in the process of creating, the level of your available energy rises, not only with respect to the specific creative activity, but to all other problems—physical, mental, emotional and spiritual.

### *How to use frustration creatively*

Frustration is always the *opportunity* for great growth, if recognized as such, and welcomed, instead of being resented. Each one of us has a great many opportunities to choose our immediate activities. The multiple pressures often become confusing, and our inability to make decisions that please everybody establishes frustrations, if the situation persists.

A positive and an infallible method of choosing an action or an activity from many possibilities, is to ask one's self, "Which of these possibilities will result in the maximum growth for myself?" In Chapter 8 we shall discuss the relationship of the recognition of the growth needs of others to our own growth needs.

Related to frustration is the inhibiting of "closure," the completing of an element of structure once begun. Closure is woven into the very fabric of the nervous system. The creative person strives for closure with great intensity. In achieving closure he has demonstrated his mastery in a situation through which he can gain the recognition he seeks and freedom from censure.

Thomas Wolfe, in describing the writing of a novel, said, "It seemed that I had inside me, swelling and gathering all the time, a huge black cloud, loaded with electricity, that had to break."

The first type of free invention occurs as a supplemental emergency defence against great anxiety. You have all noticed how much better you feel in any emergency just as soon as you start doing something.

## 6. Invent Systematically

### *Inventing is easy*

All that you have to do to be an inventor is to put together things or ideas that you have not seen together before, and which will serve some useful purpose in their new relationship. An invention is not only a new combination of old parts whose new value is the sum of its individual parts, but even more. The effect is more like a multiplication of the values of the individual parts, rather than their sum.

Something is contributed to the combination of the ideas by the mind of the inventor. Combining the controlled empirical approach with flashes of genius brings *serendipity,* the fortunate stumbling onto things of value when looking for something else. However, you will never find these unexpected treasures unless your mind is prepared to receive them, at least your subconscious mind.

Some of the greatest inventions were achieved by untrained persons who asked themselves questions. They became aware of problem areas, and were sensitive to themselves and to their limited world around them. It often happened that inventors while sensitive to problems were not sensitive to the process that they used to arrive at a solution.

Until fairly recent days an inventor could get along very well by just thinking about his problem, which would be relatively simple. Sooner or later some ideas would drift together and his problem was solved. Some of the greatest of modern inventions have been workable methods of inventiveness, and a feasible method for creative thinking.

Insight into the process of invention can increase the efficiency of any intellect in creation or problem solving. Invention by the process of purely conscious calculation seldom occurs, and yet there is a way of producing inventions in a systematic manner.

The very rapid development of new materials, new knowledge and new problems, has taken invention out of the patient plodding category. The solo inventor is just as important as ever, but he must have help.

Special inventions or innovations open up new areas of inquiry, and make many new discoveries possible. Research in the meaning of metallic conductivity resulted in the development of the transistor, which has opened a whole new world in scientific achievement that has barely been entered.

Where the magnitude of the problem warrants, room-size computers can suggest materials, designs, and methods of testing even before drawings have been made.

### *Two hundred kinds of kettles* **(Fig. 5-1 in Appendix)**

The morphological designs for electric cooking kettles and jet engines described will indicate the use of a poor man's computer, that we have chosen to call a *morphologizer.* A solo inventor can, in fifteen minutes use of the morphologizer principle, with ease suggest to himself more possible designs than many jet experts working for a week could propose, using standard procedures.

### *Nine hundred and seventy-two types of jet engines* **(Fig. 5-2 in Appendix)**

You are asked to use your imagination a little and to visualize each column of elements for the electric cooking kettle or the jet engine as being on independent vertical slides. When each of the slides has been placed in all possible relationships with all other slides the large number of possible designs is seen.

## 7. Become a Genius

***A genius is a person just like you***

If you compare, one by one, the attributes that you yourself possess with those of someone whom you consider a genius, you will find them much more alike than different. The genius has become a champion through the development of his creative potential by hard work, as does any champion. The actions of a genius are the same as any other person—carried on just a little bit farther.

As one of my college students expressed it so well, "A genius is someone who knows what he is capable of, and then urges himself to go beyond that point."

When I asked Dr. Wexler, the vice president of research for Westinghouse, to define a creative genius, he replied, "A creative genius is one who has just what my kids have." These are just the things that we have been talking about—plus a keen sense of wonder, of seeing everything as if for the first time.

The genius operates to a far greater extent on an intuitive basis than most persons. This may well be the principle reason why he *is* a genius. There appears to be little doubt that there is some kind of communication between persons beyond the ordinary six senses. Dr. Rhine of Duke University calls this Extra-Sensory Perception and has presented a great amount of evidence supporting the theory.

The real genius is a person who never lacks for ideas. They always come to him. The source of intuitive ideas has never been scientifically established. Part of them, undoubtedly, have been lying dormant, others may well have been communicated from other persons by some kind of extra sensory perception. I am sure that each of you has had the experience of playing a game of tennis or bowling with some experts, and of achieving results that far exceeded your usual standard. There is something that goes between people. One courageous person in a group that has started to panic can bring them once again to quiet and confidence.

To be a genius yourself, I am saying, put yourself in the company with as many real geniuses as you can. While I lay no claim to being a finished genius, yet I can testify from personal experience, that by interviewing more than one hundred persons who definitely were geniuses, my own creative abilities have been greatly increased. I do not know what happened, or how it happened. I just know beyond any shadow of a doubt that something good, something powerful, came to me as the result of these visits. The only satisfactory proof will be for you to try it for yourself. There are very few real geniuses who, if approached properly, will not give you a little time to help you in your efforts to think more creatively.

The genius has wisdom, which means many things. First of all wisdom means freedom from fear. It means the possession of many kinds of knowledge, knowledge gained perceptually—through the senses, knowledge gained conceptually—by subconscious combination of ideas, and knowledge gained intuitively.

### *How to be a genius*

One can *begin* to be a genius as he does the little things of everyday life. I remember one time when a secretary addressed a letter containing a check for payment of some materials to the right city but to the wrong state. This seemed like a very insignificant mistake, requiring but the addressing of a new envelope and another four-cent stamp. The secretary was puzzled at the violence of the owner's reaction until he mentioned that the $3,000 check was not now enough but must be increased to nearly $3,100 because the customary 3% discount for payment within ten days was not now deductible.

A review of the first section of Chapter 1, "You Can Be A Genius," will be quite helpful at this point, saving repetition in this chapter.

To be a genius requires faith more than anything else—faith beyond the level of understanding. The genius knows for certain, that if he responds to his inner urge to create that something worthwhile will eventually result. This holds true even if he is moving toward a goal that is neither seen nor understood. It is true, that every mental act is in some manner accompanied by a more or less perceptible atmosphere of indetermination. The poet does not know until he has written it, either what he wants to say or how he shall say it. A poem does not begin with a meaning, but as it develops what the poem is about it works toward meaning. Only when the poem has been written does the poet find out what he had to say. One poet said that it seemed as if there were a deeper understanding process which did the composing. Another writer says that creation must take place between the pen and the paper. That the creation did not take place beforehand in a thought, nor afterwards in a recasting.

If you would become a genius, then you will need to act and think like a genius. You will need to go forward in confidence and in faith that you will be directed to creative achievement.

# 6

## HOW TO GET ALONG WITH ANYBODY

***Getting along with people means to know people***

No matter how much knowledge you may accumulate, or how skillful you may become, your ultimate and lasting success will depend upon your ability to get along with people.

To get along with people means to *know* people, how they think, why they act as they do, and what their real desires are.

To know people means to be sensitive to them, to be willing to listen to what they are saying, to remember that often their words alone do not fully convey what they are really trying to say.

Regardless of position, one basic desire inherent in all men is the driving urge to be respected, through the progressive attainment of inner potentials for creative achievement.

Reduced to its very simplest terms, to get along with people means to be concerned about them, concerned about their psychological welfare as well as their finances and health. The creative person is, by nature, very sensitive to the needs and interests of others.

When I asked a director of research how he would pick out creative persons from a group he said, "I would find out to which one the others would go to talk over a problem on which they had been stuck." This attribute is more than simple technical knowledge, it also includes a genuine interest in the problems of others and a willingness, and a pleasure, in making a contribution to the solution of the problems.

***Communication and morale***

High morale in any working group is absolutely dependent on free communication. A group of five men, for example, might operate with one man as leader receiving and coordinating all ideas, with little or no communication directly between the other participants.

In another group, with the anonymity of the writers preserved, each person has the opportunity of seeing what the others had written relative to the problem under discussion.

Dr. Alex Bavelas, professor of industrial management, School of International Management at the Massachusetts Institute of Technology describes a highly enlightening experiment "Research on Communications." This study, reported in the *SOCIAL SCIENCE FOR INDUSTRY—MOTIVATION* section at the Stanford Research Institute Seminar of March 23, 1955, discusses two types of communication networks, which he calls "star" or "circle."

In the "star" type the leader occupies a position at the center of the group and communication between other members of the group is basically through the leader. This is an efficient procedure, with fewer errors but with relatively low morale on the part of group members other than the leader.

In the "circle" type, the leader is in one position on the circumference and all materials, all ideas, pass through everybody. This is a much slower procedure, more errors are made, but there is much higher morale and considerably more interest on the part of group members, resulting in a better ultimate achievement.

## 1. Develop Four-Way Communication

***Four-way communication***

In many organizations, the flow of information is from the top down—one way. In others there is a feedback to management that is of tremendous value. This is two-way communication.

While two-way communication is much better than one-way communication the feedback from the lower levels is very apt to be misleading, unless there is adequate horizontal communication. To illustrate: not infrequently one department of an organization, say design, will propose to management something that looks very good from the design point of view. Much later on when production sees the design it discovers a lot of headaches, because of unusually low tolerances, or other machine difficulties. Had production learned by the company grape-vine what was going on, and had proposed modifications, design would usually have been put in its place.

No department can live unto itself. I am aware of one concern that may well change hands because the sales manager will not speak to the production manager if he can in any way avoid it. Each is more interested in preserving his own "empire" than in asking first of all, what is best for the company. It is quite obvious that suggestions to management by either of these two department heads can not be fully depended upon.

In the ideal situation there will be completely free communication, back and forth horizontally and up and down vertically—in a four-way communication. Within each segment of an organization "circle-communication" makes the best use of personnel. Middle management should also utilize "circle-communication" in order that top management, on a policy-making level will receive *total* and accurate ideas with which to operate.

### *Communication is the final phase of creativity*

No matter how good an idea may be, it is of no value until it has been communicated to somebody able to appreciate it, and to use it. Creative persons are adept in the comunication of their ideas, probably because they are also creative in providing opportunities for communication.

The greatest thing that you have to give is your life. If some person convinces you to drop your job and to undertake something entirely different, it is very certain that he has communicated to you in a manner that you really understood. Once there was a man with an idea walking along the banks of the Sea of Galilee. He was looking for followers to help Him in His work. He approached a group of fishermen and said to them, "Come with Me, and I will make you fishers of men." His meaning was communicated instantly and very effectively, for the fishermen dropped their nets and went along.

Specialists, such as engineers, researchers, and scientists, have the problem of talking the other fellow's language. A non-technical executive will not be favorably impressed by an argument such as, "Obviously, if we take the integral of the quadratic factor, using the conjugate complex roots and rotate the covariance factor negatively, the dot vector will cancel out."

Alex F. Osborn, in his epic work, *Applied Imagination,* gives three good illustrations of communication. A salesman who called on a certain prospect for many years without making a single sale would always leave an idea each time he called. On one trip, without warning, he was handed a $100,000 order. An undergraduate who wanted to impress an interviewer from a large company went out beforehand and interviewed many of the company's dealers and competitors. During his interview he was able to offer several very worthwhile suggestions that had not come to the company's attention. While looking for a job one needs to communicate in the best way possible. The helpful organization known as LIFE-SAVERS was established to help people to get jobs. Mr. Sidney Edland, the director, stressed most heavily the importance of: (1) Offering service, and (2) Considering the interests of the prospective employer. When a personnel man hears a job candidate recognizing the needs of the company and who presents some of his qualifications that could help to fill part of these needs, the employment interviewer knows that he has before him someone quite unusual.

## 2. Work Understandingly

***What is the common objective?***

The basis for true harmony among a group working together is the unanimous acceptance of a common objective. A group of people can, if they will, find an acceptable common objective. While the many problems in a situation and their unlimited possible solutions initially may impede reaching an agreement, the possible objectives are usually distinct enough so that they may be clearly separated from one another.

The objective of one group within an automobile company to make their company the largest in the world, is readily distinguished from the objective of another group to make the best compact car in the world.

It would be impossible for the proponents of the two objectives to work harmoniously with one another. The fundamental problems of bigness are quite different from those of developing the best compact car. While of course there are many problems common to both objectives their relative importances might be widely different.

For example, a car manufacturer planning to double his output would have the problem of raw materials and accessories. It might well be very difficult for his suppliers to double their output. The compact car would require a strong research emphasis and a creative development of a brand new design. Practices and general designs that had proven quite adequate for standard cars would not do for the *new* compact car sought.

A multiplicity of strong objectives, and the lack of any dominant objective that can influence major decisions, are responsible for most business failures. Nothing can stop an organization of ten, or ten thousand people, who have a clear objective in mind and a determination to reach it.

### *How to set up an objective*

While the establishment of a company objective is the responsibility of top management, knowing these objectives is the responsibility of each employee. Those of my readers who can stand a strong shock, try bringing your own level associates together and ask each one to write down anonymously what they think are the objectives of your company. Perhaps it will then be seen why people are trying to go so many different directions at once.

What at first seem to be conflicting objectives may often be brought together in a broader objective that includes the best features of several. When this synthesis is impossible, then sometimes another department, or even another company, needs to be formed.

Let us assume that a broad objective has been set up, which is, at the same time, sharp enough to guide all major decisions. Now is the time to bring *everybody* into the picture. If the main objective has been well formulated it will be acceptable and of personal significance to each individual within the organization. The next step, that of finding problems which must be solved if the objective is to be reached is one that must directly involve those who will be faced with the problems.

### *How to find problems*

The best way to find problems in your organization is to ask the people who have them. This is effective because the man with a problem is the most anxious to have it solved. Also, it is from the persons who have problems that the solutions for those problems are to be had.

A natural question at this point is to ask why if the people who have problems also have the solutions, why don't they solve their own problems. The reason is that there are usually several people concerned with the same problem, perhaps in different ways, and each one sees and presents parts of the solution as seen from his own viewpoint.

A tested procedure, when looking for the problems that must be solved if the main objective is to be achieved, is to bring as many people together as can be effectively handled. If the size of the organization permits, bring all employees, from the president down to the low man on the totem pole into a comfortable room and seat them at tables in groups of five or six. Then, under the direction of some trained leader, perhaps from outside the company, each person should be asked to write down separately on cards, all of the problems that they can think of that are blocking the way to the attainment of their objective.

It is of extreme importance that no names, or other means of individual identification, be signed on these cards. Complete anonymity is absolutely necessary if uninhibited responses are to be obtained. Under the protecting coat of anonymity the president can be working side by side with the shipping clerk—each being stimulated by the presence of the other working on common problems.

When these problems have been synthesized by a skilled professional, the problems of each person begin to attain their full significance, as they are seen in relationship to the total problem of which they are a part.

Once the fundamental problems have been clearly set forth they may then be considered one at a time. In meetings, such as the one in which the problems themselves were derived, the ideas of every person possible—who is in any way concerned with the problem, or who may be affected by the solutions—are solicited both anonymously and publicly.

When the ideas relative to solutions for any given problem are put together and some solutions proposed, the group can work understandingly because they had the problems and also supplied the solutions. They are stimulated and increased in self-confidence because it was their problem and the solutions are also theirs, so the results will be acceptable to them, without a selling job.

### 3. Consider the Same Problem

***Cross-eyed thinking, the cause of most arguments***

At a late stage in a group discussion an argument can be of real value in selecting the best of several possible actions to solve a common problem. This, however, is not true of most arguments.

The next time you have an opportunity to listen to an argument between two people, pay very careful attention and see what the problem *really* is. In the majority of cases you will find not one, but two problems under discussion.

A salesman and the comptroller are arguing about the salesman's expense account. The comptroller points out that the expense account is the largest of any salesman in the company, and therefore must be reduced. The comptroller's problem, as he sees it, is to reduce selling costs.

The salesman, on the other hand, has been opening a new territory for the company. Competing salesmen have been very lavish in their entertainment of customers. The salesman's problem is how to get the attention of his prospects under the most favorable conditions. If dinners, shows, and ball games are what the customer is accustomed to, he will not settle for less.

The individual monthly expense account is too limited a problem. If a broader problem is put up for discussion, that will include both problems, then constructive planning can take the place of fruitless arguments. Either man might raise the question of, "What is a reasonable percentage of total selling cost to be devoted to customer entertainment?" This kind of problem calls for the gathering of accurate and complete information. Not only the comptroller and the salesman in question may contribute, but the other salesmen and other company officials. It would probably be recognized that the type of territory and the work to be done in the territory should be considered. When all available information had been synthesized and the total problem recognized, little real difficulty is usually had in arriving at mutually acceptable solutions.

### *People problems versus things problems*

The use of the family car provides another fine example of a dual problem situation. The teenage son wants the car because he is trying to solve the problem of personal status. The father is thinking about insurance costs, gasoline expense, and traffic hazards—as he considers his son's using the car. To each, his own problem is the most important.

What might be a single problem involving both the son's problems and the father's? The problem of an equitable use and support of the family car. If the son accepts his financial responsibilities he can find ways to reduce family expenses enough to make up for the added costs due to his use of the car. The father can see that status is a reasonable need of his son, as well as of the parents.

If the two parties were seeking to achieve two different objectives, they can not possibly be working on the same problem. In the car problem, *status* is not a problem, it is an objective. Security, both financial and physical, are objectives. The father was working toward two objectives and the son toward still a third objective.

Use of the car was the important part of a solution for the son, but contributed problems of cost and safety that the father feared would block his progress toward his objective. The mutual agreement by both father and son must precede any consideration of a mutual problem. If, for example, the father and son could agree on a basic family objective of usefulness, happiness and individual growth, then problems would arise when individual action would thwart the family movement toward the family objective. Considerable increase in harmony between husband and wife will always result if there is a mutual attack on common problems. It is not necessary to await a catastrophe of some kind to verify this statement.

### *Where American education is weak*

Much is written about the decrease in creativity expressed by students as their years in school increase. The school, the student, the instructor, and industry all have different objectives, and hence are trying to solve different problems. It is only in rare instances that one of these groups appreciates and respects the objectives and the problems of the others. There is nothing more vitally needed in education today, than a fusing of these diverse objectives.

The continued existence of this country may well depend upon industrial personnel doing some teaching, and instructors doing work in industry, with students working in both school and industry. In an effort to have students and instructors concerned with the same problems, through an acceptance of the same objective, various plans of alternating work and school have been tried. Antioch College and the University of Cincinnati students work six months each in college and then in industry. LeTourneau Institute, established by R. G. LeTourneau, one of this country's most controversial inventors, has an "alterday" plan, in which two students alternate each day between job and college. In this way the needs of the student, the needs of the school, and the needs of industry are brought together in one common objective.

The most pressing problems of our nation involve the solution of "people" problems, rather than "thing" problems. The time has now come when the American people must agree on some common objective that is great enough, and so well accepted by the great majority, that the size of car fins will not be considered a criterion of value in the selection of transportation.

## 4. Be Sensitive to Feedback

### *Creativity is always incomplete without feedback*

An art object is not exclusively the product of the artist, but also something to which observers react, and which is recreated through these reactions. A dramatist writes a play and a musician a score, but neither are complete until they have been transformed by actors into living performances. Creativity involves the observer, the process, and the product—as well as the creator. The criteria for the evaluation of creative achievement varies with the evaluators, the product under evaluation and the objectives of the creator.

### *Feedback can help improve human relations*

The development of improved human relations skills includes ways of dealing with conflicts and tensions. Feedback sensitivity facilitates the interaction process among participants in some group activity.

Sensitivity training attempts to close the gap between knowing and doing, to utilize both the intellectual and the emotional understanding needed for effective human relationships. Many executives glibly talk good human relations but neglect to put into practice the ideas which they proclaim. "Why don't my people ever talk back to me?" asks one manager. "Do I let them get things off their chests, or do I cut them off?"

Sensitivity training for managers is designed to develop human relations, understandings and skills and for the establishment of free and open communications.

### *Feedback gives clues to the hidden tensions of others*

It is most important to become sensitive to the ways in which people communicate to one another. "A hidden emotion expressed as a scowl on a usually sunny face tips me off that there is something wrong which needs to be corrected," was the understanding comment made to me by a store manager.

A person is most likely to see in someone else the wrongs of which he himself is guilty. Ofttimes these criticisms will bring out into the open "hidden agenda," those personal prejudices or other conditions that simmer beneath smiles and good manners.

### *Feedbacks give clues to group actions*

Feedback from the members of a group will give the receiver an understanding of group processes and group progress. It is necessary to listen carefully for the meanings and feelings expressed in group feedback. Through feedback you can learn how groups affect people and how people affect groups, thence how to help groups function more effectively.

### *Feedback from groups can serve as a mirror for self*

From feedback you can get a better picture of the kind of person that you really are, and of the kind of behaviors that you use to protect yourself from real or imagined threats. New ideas are, of course, the most frequent type of threats.

Many people tend to think in stereotypes which may drastically color their perceptions. Listening to feedback will help a person to discover some of his blind spots, those problem areas in the personality that one is often unable to perceive without gross distortion.

Understanding your own feelings and how they affect your behavior to others, and your impact on others best comes through perception of the reactions of others. Sensitivity training develops the ability to see one's self realistically, to understand one's own feelings and prejudices, and to be sensitive to the ways people relate to each other.

### *Feedbacks are therapeutic*

Often times, a word back from another will give a welcome relief from frustration, by clearing up some misunderstanding resulting from lack of knowledge. Confessions made to an uncritical, understanding person are highly therapeutic.

Receiving feedback from others will help you to indicate to yourself feelings, fears, anxieties, and other blocks that may be impeding your own progress. Such self-assessment will often lead to more self-confidence, and a feeling of real security in place of anxiety in day-by-day job relationships. You will be able to function more effectively in face-to-face situations, with individuals or before groups. Higher productivity, better morale, and lower turnover may be expected for any group, from whom feedback is received and understood.

### *A permissive atmosphere encourages feedback*

In a permissive atmosphere people feel free to speak frankly and freely, also to listen with understanding. Of course a permissive atmosphere cannot exist when the leader insists on imposing his own objectives, ideas, and methods on the group with whom he is working. In a permissive atmosphere people know that their attitudes are respected, their ideas accepted (received without immediate judgment), and full participation is facilitated.

### *How to develop sensitivity to others*

The best way to develop sensitivity to others is to really listen. To listen carefully enough so that when a speaker has finished telling you something you can repeat back his precise meaning. This is not such a simple achievement as might be supposed. The National Layman's Movement, of Rye, New York, offers a training course in Effective Listening that extends from Friday evening through Sunday noon for six weekends. The University of California at Los Angeles offers a course in sensitivity requiring eleven Wednesdays from 4:30–9:00 and one full weekend.

## 5. Respect the Fundamental Dignity of People

### *Make people feel better*

There is no more certain way of getting along with people than to have them feel better after you have touched them in some way. I have remembered for many years the instructions that my college English professor gave me as I assisted him in correcting themes and holding conferences with their writers. "Be sure to find at least two good points to commend, for every correction that is pointed out to the student."

There is probably no person who believes that he is truly perfect in any regard, and who does not actually want to improve where he is weak and defective—if he can do so without losing face. The fundamental dignity of a person is his belief in himself and his potentialities, and the probability of achieving them. People feel better when their fundamental dignity is respected. Dignity means the quality of being worthy or honorable. Fundamental means primary or original. Respect is a relationship of one person or thing to another, a motive which assists in or leads to the formation of a decision.

### *How to get the best from people*

It is quite fantastic, the many good points that any person has, if one will just look for them. This does not mean that you have to condone, or to accept, faults. But if you are sincere in wanting to improve your human relationships, looking for the good points is one absolutely sure way.

As an assignment in a class in Applied Creativity recently we asked the members of the class to find something worthy of honest commendation in the person with whom they at present "enjoyed" the worst relationship. The next week one student reported that a friction of two years' standing had been wiped away. In another week a management block of fifteen years' standing had been removed.

Respecting the fundamental dignity of a person precludes any unnecessary humiliation of that person. To humiliate a person means to make him feel low, ashamed, discouraged, and to cause uneasiness or inquietude. Rather should one attempt to glorify, to compose, to delight, to give exultation and satisfaction. Which set of attributes do you wish expressed to you by your associates, subordinates, or seniors?

Respect for another person acknowledges him to be an independent entity, as being autonomous while yet a part of his group. It means granting him full rights to his unique personality. An example of this respect is the welling pride of a man in his wife's achievements, even when they outshine his own.

### *Help people to succeed*

Success is simply a feeling, an attitude, toward one's self and his achievements, in respect to his felt purpose in life. A person who is kind, helpful, warm and respectful is a psychotherapeutic force, and people naturally gravitate to him for advice and help. A person who is approaching his real potentialities will usually treat children with real respect.

As a busy supervisor or administrator it is easy to pass over the opportunity of helping an associate to grow, to succeed. It is often overlooked that the success of a leader is measured in terms of the success of those he leads. It is impossible to promote one man until another is ready to take his place. As those under your responsibility advance, it then becomes possible for you to advance.

### *Look for the silver lining*

As difficult as it is to believe in some instances, the center of each person is inherently good. An appeal to this center, if made, cannot fail to improve your relationship toward this person. This attitude of constructive recognition has been very aptly described by Dr. Pitirim Sorokin as "Altruistic Love." This same attitude which makes a home successfully happy works equally well in business, far more effectively than an arbitrary toughness.

### 6. Be Concerned for the General Welfare

***Mutual attitudes and human relationships***

I have personally experienced so much evidence of the effects of unspoken thoughts on other people, that I am convinced that our relationships with other people depend, to a far greater extent than we realize, upon our thoughts about and our attitudes toward them.

There is much more that is not known concerning non-sensory communication than is known. However, there is little doubt that one individual acts as if he were a broadcasting station, and at the same time receiving on the same "wave length." In a large hospital I watched the recording pen of an electroencephalograph (brain wave machine) draw a line that varied with the thoughts and emotions of the patient. At Duke University I watched experiments that were determining the effects on people's minds as they transmitted thoughts to one another, and even affecting the lie of a set of dice.

For many years I have been aiding college physics students to become free from the common difficulty of "freezing up" in examinations, when they were in reality well prepared. The students were instructed to see their subject matter as operating in the service of others. It is *self*-consciousness that blocks the flow of knowledge. As one cannot be self-conscious and *other*-conscious at the same time, thinking of the welfare of others will release in great profusion the creative power within. Try this for yourself, it will never fail to work.

The development and maintenance of an altruistic attitude toward one's associates is so easy to do, and the results are so striking, that we hope that you will make the effort to try it—starting with the person with whom you have the poorest relationship. There is no defense against good thoughts. The other person can not help improving his attitude and his relationship toward you if your own attitude is improved.

### *Developing mutual concern in an organization*

Getting along means the existence of mutual concern. If one person in a group has as his major concern his own self-advancement, this objective may well conflict with that of another person striving for the same goal. The higher one rises in an organization the more vicious becomes the competition and the fewer the opportunities for self-advancement.

In a certain home appliance factory the production manager receives an annual bonus based solely on the number of appliances that his department produces. Whether or not the company was able to make any money on the appliances produced had no bearing on the size of the bonus. During one year the company as a whole lost money because of the production manager's poor judgment; so much so that it had to borrow the money to pay the production manager's bonus. This self-objective of the production manager to make all the money he could at the expense of the rest of the company—officials and employees—was beyond doubt the basic cause of the dissention in the company. The resulting lack of communication is the reason for the many blunders made.

A business does not exist primarily for the benefit of any single person, no matter what his position may be. If an objective accepted by one individual would inhibit the progress of others in an organization, it certainly can not be the best objective.

It is not reasonable to expect one individual to support activities that will block his progress toward his own objective, just to further your progress.

What is best for the company, is a question that encourages an harmonious association. What is best for me usually causes friction and lessened harmony among individuals. If, instead of separate and individual objectives for the members of an organization, there is set up a general objective whose attainment will be for the benefit of all associated individuals, there will then be no reason for any refusal to cooperate.

### *Love thy neighbor*

There has never been any better advice for getting along with people than that expressed in the great decalog. Too often this advice is looked upon as a one-way process. This is most certainly not the case. If we use for our definition of love the concern for the welfare of others, and accept the idea that one cannot receive love without giving it back, or better, sharing it, then the two-way concept is reasonable.

There are so many people around you that your opportunities for contributing are without limit, as are the returns. A pond that retains all water that flows into it soon becomes stagnant. So does a personality that constantly takes in and refuses to give out.

One method of acquiring data on radio or television programs that are tuned in at any given time is based on the fact that any receiver is also radiating on the same frequency. A truck going along the street can point a highly sensitive directional microphone at one antenna after the other, as it drives along the street, and tell what program is being received in a home.

A wish that somebody would fail miserably in some task attempted so that you then could come into the picture and do the job successfully may be so strongly received as to cause that person to fail. The same radiations are being returned to you and can cause your own subsequent failure.

### *Getting and losing jobs*

Extensive studies at Harvard University, and at other institutions, have clearly shown that a failure to get along with one's associates is the primary cause for the loss of jobs, far exceeding any lack of technical skill.

Most people are hired because somebody believes that their services will contribute to the success of a business.

### *Creativity and concern*

The creative personality almost always has a sincere desire to help mankind. I do not pretend to understand just *how* an outgoing concern for others releases the creative forces dormant within, but I know that it does. Try this for yourself the next time that you are called upon to give a talk. Instead of thinking about the personal effect you are making consider what you may be able to do for your audience. You can not possibly be stage struck unless you are concentrating on yourself.

***"Try Giving Yourself Away"***

Some twenty years ago, David Dunn wrote a little book called *Try Giving Yourself Away* that so beautifully expresses the spirit of what I have tried to say in this chapter that each one of you is most strongly urged to find a copy and to read it. David Dunn discovered the secret of a thrilling life by expressing his sincere concern for the welfare of others, in many little acts of service and appreciation.

## 7. Strive to Increase Good Will

***The meaning of good will***

Good will is a very complicated attribute of personality. It means the potential response of others to your reputation, to the image that you have built up. Good will is, in part, the climate about you in which others react. The type of response characterized by good will has the attributes of an upright disposition or intention, sincerity, readiness, cheerful consent, heartiness, kindly feeling and cheerful acquiescence. Perhaps the one word *favorable* may best describe the total nature of good will.

Good will is manifested in a group as well as in individual behavior. Certainly today nations of the world are keenly sensitive to international friendliness and good will as never before. Group behavior, readiness, and zeal reflect the degree of goodwill of a group toward its leaders.

***How to develop good will***

The establishment of an image of yourself, or of your organization in the minds of people such that their natural response would reflect good will, requires planned efforts. To begin with, it is necessary to display toward others the same aspects of good will that you desire them to display toward you. Attributes of good will include: good intention or inclination, kindly regard, toleration, cordiality, kindliness, consideration, generosity, geniality, a sense of humor, sympathy, honesty, guilelessness, and an open mind.

# 7

## HOW TO HELP OTHERS BE CREATIVE

***Creative assistance is a two-way service***

Helping others to be creative is just as much for the benefit of the helper as for the helped. No one person in an organization has all of the knowledge required to operate its affairs successfully. Total participation makes possible the utilization of differences of opinion instead of being frustrated by them.

When cooperation for the good of all is substituted for divisive competition, the creative achievement of the entire group is raised. In helping others to be creative, through respecting the need for every person to achieve his own potential, your own success is made more certain. Moreover, the resistance to a new idea or to the solution of a problem, is lessened according to the number of persons who have contributed to the idea or the solution.

The cultural aids to creativity, although usually more quiet and easily overlooked, are much more numerous and in reality stronger than the cultural blocks to creativity. There are many new aids to communication, such as *air page* for example. On the hour I can receive on my little pocket radio a personal message from my office telling me about some urgent matter needing my attention.

There is another and equally important side to communication, the intuitive or feeling side. Freedom of expression may be had from the members of any group only when there is freedom from fear of reprisal, through complete anonymity.

## 1. Get Everybody Into the Act

***Success depends on the use of personal powers***

Lack of business capital is not the basic cause of business failure. The primary reason is the refusal of top management to recognize the need to utilize fully the knowledge and experience of all employees.

The greatest waste in America is the failure to use the available creative power—the intellectual and the intuitive. In any organization there is almost always the knowledge and the experience necessary for success.

While it is quite likely that the president of an organization, especially if he has worked his way up from the bottom, may know more about the business than any other person in the organization, his knowledge, understanding and experience are always far less than the sum total of the entire organization.

Powerful forces operate within an organization to keep it moving in smooth and familiar paths. These frequently are brought to bear on any individual who tries to introduce a new idea which is potentially a disrupting influence. It is customary to resist change, and group activity is the best antidote to organizational inertia.

If an idea is presented as the product of a group, rather than that of an individual, the additional weight and prestige is more successful in bringing ideas to the point of implementation.

***Freedom through group thinking***

Group thinking is the surest way to enable an individual to become free from the thinking patterns he has built up.

Audible group discussions are very often productive of helpful ideas, but only if three requirements are observed: (1) the problem must be quite limited in scope, (2) the topic of discussion is non-controversial, (3) the participants are of the same general level or status.

It is frequently very difficult for many people to express themselves verbally, especially where part of the group is hostile or prejudiced. If participants in a working group are invited to write their ideas on cards, or slips, complete freedom of reply is enjoyed. Also, it is good for the morale of a company if all personnel—from the president down to the youngest employee—are seated around tables working together on problems of common significance. If you are seated at a table with four or five other people who are busily writing down ideas, the pressure on you will be strong. You will do your utmost to come up with some ideas of your own so as not to be looked upon as an "odd-ball."

### *Strive for total group participation*

There is absolutely no sense to the controversy on individual versus group invention. It is similar to asking what is the most important item, the airplane that takes a person up into the air, or the parachute that brings him down to earth when he jumps out of the airplane for the sport of jumping. While the process of synthesis is essentially individualistic, it may occur simultaneously in several minds. A greater variety of ideas, submitted by several persons, will make possible a broader concept than one person could possibly achieve had he worked entirely alone. An individual inventor, or problem solver, may offer as his solution one that meets only a part of the specific set of conditions that should be considered. The more people who contribute ideas relative to a problem, the more likely that all specifications and elements will be available for consideration and synthesis.

It is also quite true, that the more individuals there are who can see their ideas reflected in the pattern of the final solution, the fewer objections will be raised against the solution.

Scientists, who are frequently caught at their own frontiers, will want to meet other workers who have been similarly caught on their own frontiers. Together, after a sharing of ideas, both are able to make further progress.

On the size of an organization, or the number of persons affected, rests the decision on whether to ask for the ideas of all individual members, or from a representative cross section. In selecting the people to participate in problem-solving activities it is my policy to seek to have representatives of every type of person who will be affected by the solution that is finally adopted. If the problem were the design of a new washing machine, not only would the designers participate, but the sales department, the distributors and maintenance people, and especially the customers who would use the new machine.

### *The effect of the environment on participation*

To get everybody into the act of solving some problem requires the establishment of an environment in which participation will not only be free from pain, but actually enjoyable because the opportunity and the encouragement of creative expression is present. The organizational obstacle course for new ideas is chiefly responsible for organizations and businesses falling behind their competitors.

The failure of formal education to bring out the creative talent of students is partially due to the disproportionate use of the method of *analysis,* which underlies scientific training, to the exclusion of the method of synthesis as employed in the process of invention.

Cheating in examinations is considered to be one of the greatest problems worrying educators. It is not cheating that is the real problem but the failure to recognize that the enforced isolation of examinations is unnatural. On the job, difficult problems always require the sharing of information.

While some of the aptitudes which have an important influence are hereditary, the majority are subject to development under proper environmental circumstances. Most engineers possess a creative spark which does not develop naturally. At the General Electric Company, A. C. Spark Plug Company and many other institutions, it has been shown conclusively that with the right environment creativity can be developed.

## 2. Utilize Differences of Opinion

### *How to disagree constructively*

When two or more persons discuss any subject whatever, there are bound to be differences of opinion, if each one is completely honest and honestly complete. There are really but two ways of handling differences of opinion, either to keep fighting until one opinion rises triumphantly on top, or to make a sincere attempt to utilize multiple viewpoints.

Conflicting ideas may in reality be in close harmony, not necessarily with each other, but with the particular problem that is in the mind of the proponent of each of the ideas.

The complaint department in a department store, or the public relations department of a large corporation, may be so operated as to pay dividends. The basic difference between the two seems to be that the complaint department waits until something has gone wrong while the public relations department goes out among its clients looking for ways to improve the institutional image, as well as to become sensitive to things that should be corrected.

### *Creative tolerance*

The creative person is unhappy with the conditions that he finds around him but has what may be termed constructive discontent. He can tolerate the unsatisfactory conditions and be experiencing happiness in his attempts to improve them. He is tolerant toward persons with different interests, motives, ideals and abilities. The creative person is especially understanding in his attitude toward his less creative associates.

Related to the individual's capacity to tolerate ambiguity is sensitivity. Even though the creative individual is existing in a state of affairs where he does not consciously comprehend all that is going on, yet intuitively he continues to effect resolution of the problem confronting him.

A sharp lesson to parents is the undisputed fact that people who have tolerant personalities have come from homes where security is felt by the members of that home, and where the use of threats is very rare.

Tolerant people tend to show mental flexibility and sensitivity because there is no sharp cleavage between their conscious and subconscious attitudes and processes. They have achieved a large measure of synthesis and mutual support of sensory and intuitive stimuli and processes. It is difficult to find a man who is tolerant of people and who is not also open to new ideas, and tolerant to those that differ from his own.

### *Look for the hidden agenda*

Members of a group who carry on stubborn attacks on other members or their ideas, or strongly support ideas which have nothing to do with the main issue, often have "hidden agendas." They are seeking to build their own power or prestige or are attempting to defeat the actual goal of the group without appearing to oppose it.

It might well be recognized that every person in any group has at least some measure of a "hidden agenda," something that is more for his own benefit than for the group's. The more close an agreement, and the more acceptance of the general objective of the best for the group, the less apt there are to be determining "hidden agendas." Sensitivity to hidden agendas, and their natures, provides clues to probable objections to be anticipated and sublimated. The persistent attempt to switch the discussion from the true topic is a sure clue to the "power jockey."

## 3. Substitute Cooperation for Misguided Competition

### *Cooperation through a common objective*

Objectives arising out of consideration for personal, individual, benefits must result in misguided competition. Cooperation and friendly competition result when an all-inclusive objective, one that is for the ultimate good of the entire organization is accepted. With one common objective everybody wins.

A guiding objective that is acceptable to all concerned can only be developed if there is cognizance of the needs and desires of all affected by the objective.

Of course simply talking about an ideal objective will avail little or nothing unless management and supervision clearly indicate by their *actions* that what is best for the organization as a whole is also the best for each individual. The manager of production, mentioned in a previous chapter, who accepted a bonus, even though due to his errors in judgment his company had lost money and had to borrow his bonus money from the bank, is a glaring example of the fruits of misguided competition.

### *Freedom through cooperation in terms of a common objective*

The establishment of a common objective stimulates cooperation because it gives more freedom for every member of the group than does individual objectives. This might seem to be a highly conflicting statement, but if management knows that all personnel are striving for a common objective, it is willing to permit more individuality in procedures, both in the performance of specific tasks and in the solving of problems.

Working, with appropriate recognition, toward a common objective restores to personnel part of the deep creative satisfaction that has been lost by the majority of employees, as automation has replaced artistic expression in the products of skilled hands.

### *A common objective makes a strong management—not a stubborn one*

The establishment of a common objective is, of course, completely dependent on free communication, the four-way communication discussed in Chapter 6. It is not enough for the boss to say that his door is always open to any employee, his mind must be equally open to the ideas of his employees, *before* he makes up his mind.

An executive will find out that his decisions are better and more acceptable when more individuals contribute their own views. By virtue of his over-all responsibility, the chief executive can not have the necessary detailed information to make decisions, unless others give him the benefit of their knowledge and experience.

There are people whose contributions are largely sensory, dealing with things seen, heard, and touched. But equally as important are those people for whom the realm of the intuition provides the indispensible power and synthesis, without which ultimate failure for any undertaking is inevitable.

If management makes certain that all personnel have one common objective, which has been universally accepted throughout the organization, then will management not only receive *more* ideas, upon which to base its decisions, but *better* ones.

### *Recognition as a stimulus to cooperation*

Among the basic needs of all persons are self-respect and the esteem of others. Self-respect involves personal strength, achievement, adequacy, mastery, competence, independence and freedom. The esteem of others entails reputation, prestige, status, dominance, recognition, importance and appreciation.

These attributes of self-respect and the esteem of others are enhanced by cooperative actions. It is, therefore, of paramount importance that all persons be given as much recognition as possible. It costs so little and means so much.

Having the esteem of one's associates is a natural, an innate desire. This is one of the strongest desires, or urges that we possess. If we do not have the desired esteem, *or if we think we do not,* which is more often the case, we then take defensive measures.

The simplest and the most common reaction, if we feel a lack of the esteem of others, is to claim that we do not want it. We either withdraw ourselves from contact with those whose esteem we really want, or so conduct ourselves that those persons could not possibly have much respect or esteem for us.

If we are too painfully conscious of a disparity between our own worthiness for high esteem and that of others, and do not wish to make the effort to increase our position, it is quite simple to try to drag others down closer to our own level. There are examples of this type of person in all fields. In writing, we have that prosperous gang of muckrakers who devote their entire sordid lives in attempts to degrade the reputation and to lessen the influence of Washington, Lincoln, and many others who, on occasion, had lacked the perfection that none of us have attained. It is almost impossible to still the lying lips or to stop the poisonous pen of these greedy sensation-mongers, who intentionally develop false concepts in the minds of men by the presentation of isolated facts, taken out of context—including their times in cultural history.

We who are concerned with the welfare of our country, and of the entire world, can and must combat the effects of these traitorous pollutants of our culture. We must give full and free recognition to all the good things that people do. It is not even necessary that we know these people personally. Our words will be even more meaningful if we are strangers to them.

May I again most strongly recommend the reading of David Dunn's little classic, *Try Giving Yourself Away*. The tremendous outpouring of creative achievement that will always come from persons who feel that they are genuinely appreciated, and the total absence of cost in expressing this appreciation, makes one wonder why it is so hard for most people to give freely or to accept graciously expressions of appreciation.

## 4. Provide Anonymity to Members of Non-Homogeneous Groups

***How to use manpower effectively***

The people in any organization are its most important assets, and the most difficult to replace. One of the principle responsibilities of management is to achieve the maximum return from its investment in people.

Not only must there be clear channels of communication throughout an organization, if full utilization of brain-power is to be had, but people must understand and believe that their full participation is really desired by management and supervision.

Once an entire organization is convinced that their full participation is sincerely desired, what more must be done to make this participation become a reality? Earlier in this chapter we spoke of the importance of recognition of contributions in relation to the consideration of the esteem of others. Right now we are concerned with getting the ideas expressed in the first place.

The intellectual resources of most organizations have scarcely been touched, and the cumulative experience barely used. It is well known that the man who makes the most noise in a conference is not necessarily the man with the best ideas. Often, after the conference has broken up, one of the quiet men will casually mention an original idea of exceptional merit. The simple answer to the problem of getting hold of the good ideas of the quiet people is complete anonymity, at least during a part of the conference. The "organization man" can then loudly proclaim what he believes the man who can promote him wants to hear, in open session, and can then say what he really believes, or feels, while fully protected.

The providing of complete anonymity is very simply achieved by the use of small cards or slips of paper. For a number of reasons I have found a plain white card that is three inches long and two and one-half inches wide is very satisfactory. In a conference each person is handed a supply of these cards and is requested to write one idea per card concerning the topic under consideration. Not only does this procedure offer the participants the maximum opportunity for free expression, but management itself is protected from inadequate decisions based on incomplete information.

### *Anonymity releases intuitive power*

Why does the quiet man remain quiet, and why is it so important for him to release his ideas? The quiet man is often an intuitive thinker, who is not limited by—nor dependent on—the sensory stimulants to which most of his associates react. The quiet man has learned, from bitter experience, that if he offers an idea that is different from the usual pattern expressed by the group he will be attacked vigorously, and that he will often be made to appear at a disadvantage during the battle because he may not know *why* his idea is a good one.

To get the break-through ideas of the quiet man, or the deep-seated emergent ideas of the more outspoken members of the group which they feel but refuse to express openly, protection must be afforded against the roughshod tactics considered to be appropriate to most conferences. Anonymity gives complete protection and also freedom to fail. Fear of failure is beyond any doubt the greatest inhibitor of creative expression. Anonymity, then, beyond releasing the intuitive powers of individuals, will increase the confidence, the intuitive power, and the achievement of the group.

### *Anonymity makes non-homogeneous groups more effective*

While the low-salaried employee may have relatively less power to change undesirable conditions, he most certainly is closer to the actual problems affecting the success of the organization to which he belongs. In most situations, an executive will receive from his associates the kind of suggestions which the executive is thought to desire. This is especially true of the well-trained "organization man."

When complete anonymity is provided, personalities disappear and ideas must stand on their own merit. It is quite obvious that an idea known to be in accord with the views of the president would be apt to receive more consideration than one offered by a shipping clerk. This would be true even though the problem involved were in the shipping department, and one with which the clerk was intimately involved.

In oral conferences if a member of top-level management is present, even though he refrains from audible comment, his expressions are evidence enough to the careful observer of the official reaction to ideas presented. There is no other way to obtain complete participation of all members of an organization than to preserve complete anonymity at times.

## 5. Lessen Resistance to New Ideas

### *Good ideas are sure to be resisted*

In order to be creative a person must express his ideas in the solution of problems. Creative expression is such a strong urge that, if repressed, actual suffering results. Nevertheless, the satisfaction from creative achievement, once experienced, is sufficient to cause the creative person to accept hardship, opposition, and even persecution—gladly and willingly.

If the idea that you advance is any good at all, somebody affected is certain to object. The better your idea, the more resistance you may expect. If nothing else will stop you, somebody may try to kill you.

### *Reasons and excuses for opposing new ideas*

Our concern at this point is *why* people usually object to new ideas, and what can be done about this common tendency.

New ideas are resisted vigorously because of fear, or laziness, or both. The fear of the unknown, of the new, is continuously increasing among men, because of an increase in the amount of sensory stimuli and a decrease in sensitivity to intuition.

One reasonable objection for the customary resistance to new ideas is the fact that the acceptance and the implementation of but *one* new idea will make necessary the re-evaluation and the modification of many ideas and concepts that have served well for years. Take for example a chain bank that has grown from a few branches to many. The head office can no longer respond to calls from the branches for decisions as quickly as the branches of competing banks with more independent branches. The paternalistic home office control is forced, against its will, to consider the idea of decentralization. Many issues now arise that concern the bank's top management. First, there is the reluctance of any executive to surrender any part of his authority; second, there is a real concern as to the capabilities of branch management to assume and to handle successfully the new responsibilities, which an increase in branch autonomy would develop.

Those responsible, at the home office, for the financial security of the bank are naturally reluctant to allow others to make decisions for which home office officials are held responsible by the board of directors and the stockholders.

The home office has had new responsibilities thrust upon it by the acceptance of the basic idea of decentralization. It must see that branch management acquires the added understanding it will need. There must be developed a far better four-way system of communication, as discussed in Chapter 6.

***Understanding creative people***

The typical person when confronted with a new idea first of all tries to find out what is *wrong* with it. If he can find enough things wrong with it so that his group will discard the idea, he is happy, because he then will not have to do something that is different from that which he has been doing.

The true scientific approach is an intuitive process, that of business and industry largely intellectual. Business analyzes, science synthesizes. Science will *receive* an intuitive suggestion and ask what would it mean if the new idea were true. If the possibilities seem interesting enough, some scientist will follow it through.

I have been told directly by many of this country's greatest scientists, and other creative achievers, that they have never made any significant advance, any breakthrough, without appealing to and then following the suggestions of their intuition.

Those responsible for the treatment and the utilization of highly effective people, especially in the field of research, should fully realize that these people are unable to tell for what purposes many of their ideas may be utilized. They had been given the idea intuitively and expressed it so that it would not be lost, but might not have any intellectual justification for it at all. As mentioned earlier in this book, the director of research of the Westinghouse Corporation justified a reasonable amount of unstructured seeking for two main reasons: (1) when a real tough "company" problem has to be solved, nobody but the curious seeker of the new for its own sake could solve them, and (2) the company had found that the new ideas brought back from these intellectual "joy rides," when finally applied, have made possible such significant advances as to have paid for their costs many times over.

An idea that has been intuitively conceived and developed is very often difficult to substantiate intellectually.

At many of the scientific laboratories that I have visited I was told that most of their products just now going on the market could have been ready five or ten years ago. The necessary knowledge was in existence but somebody had been squelched and the idea ploughed under. While an idea must eventually be carefully evaluated prior to being acted upon, too prompt judgment and rejection is to blame for America's greatest waste of good ideas.

***What you yourself can do to lessen resistance to your ideas***

Most of the resistance to new ideas may be *sublimated,* not overcome, through the utilization of the principles and methods presented in the preceding four sections of this chapter.

The proponent of a new idea can reduce *initial* resistance if he will refrain from the discussion of problems and methods. No management, unless operating on a cost plus basis, would ever oppose the idea of a department head to reduce costs of his department by ten per cent.

The reason for this lack of objection is a basic one that is often, I will even say usually, missed by middle managment and by supervision. Cost reduction is an *objective,* not a problem or a solution. It is possible to so state any objective that is for the good of an organization that little or no objections will be raised. This is because nothing has to be done, no methods have to be changed, just as the result of listening to an objective.

The second phase would be naming the problems that must be solved to achieve the goal of a ten per cent reduction in department costs. If all persons interested or concerned in any way are invited to mention problems as they see them from various viewpoints, there again need be little contention, especially if no solutions are presented during this phase.

The third phase of problem solving, that of suggesting actual solutions, will be far more harmonious if all persons are attempting to solve the *same problem.* By the proper handling of all suggestions offered and including them in the report of group action, each person can see that his ideas have been considered and evaluated. The final proposal will then have as part of its foundation the contributions of the entire group. Any objections raised are then, in part, being raised against the objector's own ideas.

Just because you are, yourself, fully aware of an existing problem, does not mean that the recipient of any ideas that you may offer relative to the problem is, himself, aware of the problem. Much time is wasted in proposing methods of solution when the

some people increases their frustration, for others it calls forth enough extra effort to use the difficulty instead of being bruised by it.

Self-realized persons waste less of their time and energy protecting themselves against their own actions, and from their own thoughts.

A person whose basic motivation is growth is psychologically free. If concern about meeting deficiencies is paramount, then he is a psychological slave.

## 7. Utilize Environmental Stimulators of Creativity

***Every felt need stimulates creativity***

When relationships between the various areas of living and their common problem areas are pointed out, many creative questions immediately arise. In this section we shall simply indicate how creative questions may be raised that will stimulate creative action.

In Chapter 2 we discussed the *Principal Areas of Living* and the *Problem Systems* common to all of them. While other areas and problem systems might be used, these are so universally appreciated that they were selected for our use.

| AREAS OF LIVING | PROBLEM SYSTEMS |
|---|---|
| A. SELF | A. FINANCE |
| B. FAMILY | B. DISCIPLINE |
| C. OCCUPATION | C. HEALTH |
| D. COMMUNITY | D. ESTEEM-POWER |
| E. COUNTRY | E. EDUCATION |
| F. WORLD | F. COMMUNICATION |
| G. CHURCH | G. RECREATION |

If each of the areas of living were to be paired with each of the problem areas there would result 49 different kinds of relationships, each being a powerful stimulator of creativity. Because of space limitations we shall indicate but seven, one for each area of living. One relationship being as good as another, for purposes of illustration, we shall arbitrarily relate area of living (A) to problem system (A), (B) with (B), (C) with (C), etc.

***Finances of the individual***

How may one be more certain of receiving full value for the money expended for goods and services?

What better way of handling personal finances may be used than the use of credit cards?

***Family discipline***

In what ways may the improvement of adult discipline aid in better child discipline?

How may improved family discipline lead to greater enjoyment for the whole family on extended automobile trips?

In what ways may improved family discipline increase family harmony and individual freedom?

***Your job and your health***

In what ways may the physical health conditions of your job be improved?

How may unnecessary mental strain be reduced in amount and intensity?

In what ways may unnecessary physical strains be eliminated in the lifting or moving of heavy objects?

An inventor of my acquaintance, after frequently being squirted with oil from the joints in the lines of a high pressure hydraulic press, developed a fluid that was neither a liquid nor a gas and that could not possibly leak. He mixed small steel ball bearings and flaked graphite, creating a new fluid that worked perfectly—and for which he has now received a basic patent.

***Our country and education***

How may the type of thinking permitted in schools and colleges more nearly parallel the kind of thinking that is now necessary, if our country is to survive in its life and death struggle with communism?

How may schools engender a greater appreciation of the mutual concern for general welfare as a prerequisite for individual welfare?

### *The community and esteem-power*

What can be done in the community in order that the self-respect, and the esteem by others, of all citizens may be enhanced?

In what ways may the desire for power on the part of many political leaders be more in harmony with the needs of people?

### *World communication*

How may the people of one country know the truth about the people of another country?

In what ways may the people of one country communicate directly with the people of another country without having their communications polluted by self-centered political influences?

### *The church and recreation*

What type of recreational program may the church offer that will present more than a cleaned-up version of the standard commercial and secular variety?

# 8

## HOW TO MAKE GOOD DECISIONS

***Making decisions is an unavoidable responsibility***

The making of decisions is one responsibility that none of us can escape. Even if we plan on having someone else make our decisions for us, we still have to decide on whose decisions we are willing to accept.

Any good decision is one that considers all of the elements involved in a situation, and their total complex of relationships. To be certain that you are considering the total situation, you will not confine your ideas to those gained by your own efforts—you will seek as varied viewpoints as is possible.

One source of information that you may frequently overlook is yourself. Somehow we have a tendency to value the ideas of another person more than our own. Even if the decision involves technical knowledge that you do not have, your own intuition will often suggest valuable ideas to be incorporated in any decision to be made.

A fundamental requirement for sound decisions is a certainty that a series of proposals, from which you must select the one to be adopted, all refer to the same problem.

The reduction of mental stress on the part of contributors, whose ideas are to form the meat for your decision, will result in more and better ideas.

Finally, if you would make good decisions, beware of false values, such as buying a car because it has big fins or horsepower.

## 1. Determine the Basic Pattern of a Situation

***Recognize the dynamic pattern in a situation***

The ultimate requirement for the making of a good decision is a clear, comprehensive view of the total situation. It is not enough to know thoroughly the specific elements of the situation; their manifold and complex relationships also need to be seen and understood.

A certain large manufacturer of air-conditioning equipment needed to know which of three possible general types of heat pumps they should manufacture and sell, if they were to maintain their place in this highly competitive business.

The basic pattern of the situation, from which the final decision may be made is shown in Figure 8-1. If all of the components shown are considered in all possible relationships, then a good decision is probable. Such a display of the field of decision is the *end* result of the morphological process, to be discussed in the remaining six sections of this chapter.

It should be remembered that the several parameters shown are to be thought of as being on separate slides. When the seven slides have been placed in *all* possible positions in relation to each other there will have been seen nearly 80,000 different relationships.

***Why pattern decisions are better (see Fig. 8-1 in Appendix)***

There were three types of heat pumps under serious consideration: the split, the integral, and the combination known as the split-integral. In the split type there were separate units for heating and cooling, placed at different locations, and connected up by local labor on the job. The unit type had both heating and cooling units combined at the factory, completely assembled. The split integral was intended to be adapted to either of the two types of installations. The split-integral combination was soon shown to be undesirable, so our discussion here will deal only with the first two types mentioned.

Imagine yourself as one of an executive board that has to make the decision between the two types of heat pumps. Such a financial board is not apt to be composed of highly technical men, but the matter as presented to them must enable the board to make a decision that is in harmony with technical truths.

When discussed under the parameters of installation, dependability, development and cost, the integral unit was far superior to the unit type, and seemed obviously to be the better of the two. But when the sales manager raised the question as to which type would sell the most units—the integral unit—even though less costly and more dependable, became less desirable because of the space required. Very few homes had room in their structure for the integral type.

This changed the picture completely. The decision was made to manufacture and sell both types, meanwhile carrying on an educational campaign with architects and home builders to provide room for the better, lower cost, and cheaper maintenance of the integral type.

### *How to make practical use of 80,000 ideas*

Persons who have been accustomed to making a choice from a very small number of ideas, are frequently completely bewildered when confronted by a number of ideas that may reach 80,000 or more, as did the heat pump decision. What is a person to do? It would take at least two months to consider them all, if even three minutes were spent on each relationship.

I asked Dr. Zwicky this question, "What to do with 80,000 ideas?" His suggestion was that the decision maker ask himself, "What is the 'king' value?"

In the case of the heat pump problem, the "king" value was to sell as many heat pumps as possible at a profit, and soon enough to maintain their staff of salesmen, installers, production workers, and maintenance men. The great preponderance of data pointed positively at the integral type as being the best choice.

But when the "king" value was considered, the decision involving a compromise was quite obvious.

## 2. Utilize Multiple Viewpoints

### *Incomplete points of view result in bad decisions*

There are two schools of thought among manufacturers. One expects the sales department to sell what can be made. The other endeavors to make what can be sold.

Had the heat pump company been of the first type, the sales department might never have seen the final product until it was ready to be sold. In this case the serious effects on sales of the space requirements might well have been missed, until too late to have determined production and choice of type. Fortunately for this company, the viewpoint of the salesman was considered early enough so that the space element was seen in its true significance.

In addition to the salesmen and the company designers, other persons involved in sales were used as data sources. The customer, the distributors, the competitors, the market were all considered in relationship to the "king" value, as well as to the material aspects of the heat pump.

Getting information by the use of methods involving anonymity proved of considerable value in getting complete and honest expressions from the various persons affected by the decision to be made. A more complete discussion of the use of anonymity is given in Chapter 7, Section 4.

Strange as it may seem, most people do not like to receive ideas that will force them to change their intended plans. They would rather use a familiar—though inferior—plan, and resent any suggestions to the contrary. The complete concept that is possible through the use of anonymity of response enables this kind of person to see the total picture before making an audible decision. He is then permitted to change his position without feeling that he has "lost face" by so doing.

There is another very important result from the use of multiple viewpoints, and that is the greatly stimulated personal interest of those given the opportunity to participate in the formulation of a decision. Interest and acceptance is especially keen if the contributor can see the effect of some suggestion of his in the end result.

***Reducing risks in decision making***

The utilization of multiple viewpoints greatly minimizes the risk in making decisions, both because of the greater number of ideas available, and also because the persons concerned will more actively look for dangers to the plan adopted if their ideas are utilized.

While management may delegate *authority* it can never delegate its *responsibility*. Management's chief responsibility is to make *decisions*. The principal responsibility of everyone other than management is to provide the *material* for decisions—not to make them.

## 3. Consider All of the Essential Elements

***How to reduce the risks of bad decisions***

All types of decisions can very easily come to grief if some fundamental elements are neglected. The initial decision in favor of the integral heat pump had to be greatly modified when the sales department raised the issue of the availability of space in existing structures to house the integral heat pump.

A decision, to be sound, and to present the minimum risk, must utilize all available information seen in as many relationships as possible. It is unlikely that there would be any serious disagreement with the foregoing statement, but the principle involved is very often disregarded in the process of making decisions.

Not too long ago all airplanes of a certain model were grounded because the wings started falling off. This was quite embarrassing to the pilot, because it was really not his fault at all.

Had one very simple principle, that of resonance, been considered, the entire difficulty could have been avoided. For the benefit of my readers who have forgotten their physics, resonance means the reception of pulses of energy in time with the natural rate of motion of a body. A child in a swing absorbs the energy of a series of small shoves faster than it dissipates the energy while swinging. The result is an accumulation of energy and a very large amplitude of swing.

One of the initial shocks to a new rider in an airplane occurs when he notices how much the wing tips bend up and down as the plane moves through rough weather. The wing, in common with any vibrating body, has its own natural rate of vibration, which is constant. If the wing receives a continued series of even moderate stresses *in resonance* with the natural rate of vibration, the amount of wing flutter will become larger and larger. If the amplitude becomes large enough the wing will break off, as some have done, even though actually loaded far below their safe stress from any conceivable single shock.

An extensive investigation finally brought out the fact that vibrations set up by the engines at certain speeds were picked up by the wings that had the same natural frequency. In order to permit the planes to continue flying safely, they were required to fly at a lower speed at which the dangerous engine-caused vibrations were absent, and the wings then remained intact.

The latest and best computers in existence had proven conclusively that no possible combinations of normal flight stresses could possibly result in wing failure. There were no mistakes in the complicated mathematics utilized. The designers had simply neglected to consider the normal vibration rate of the wings in relationship to other vibrations set up in the frame of the airplane that might be in resonance with the wing frequency.

### *How to handle a thousand suggestions*

A consideration of the essential elements must include a consideration of as many as possible of the relationships of the elements. In the heat pump decision, all of the indisputable facts of research and development indicating that the integral heat pump was far superior to the unit type became of minor immediate significance when seen in relationship to the difficulty of installation in existing buildings.

In order to consider all of the essential elements of a problem, these elements must be on display—shown in such a way that the relationships between the elements can be seen readily. The heat pump morphologram given in Figure 8-1 (in Appendix) illustrates how this may be done.

It is well to remember, at this point, that the heat pump display was not the result of an analysis (taken in the most usual sense of dividing up) of the total problem.

Several hundred small cards, each one presenting one idea by a single person who would be affected by the final decision, were laid out in blocks of twelve. Then by a process of *synthesis,* to be described in Chapter 9, all of the cards were finally *combined* into the parameters and the components shown. The analysis of the problem resolves itself into the simple separation of the total problem into the components or parameters shown along natural cleavage lines. The components of each parameter are given deeper significance because their over-all relationships are constantly kept in mind with the total display.

*Every* idea submitted by *anyone* was included in the display of the heat pump problem. Elements that did not fit easily in the earlier groupings were put into separate groupings, without any forcing. Under this procedure, one single card that contained an off-beat idea was brought into a sharp focus. This is often the idea that points the way to a daringly new and highly valuable solution.

### *How to verify the completeness of information available*

One great advantage of the morphological display of a problem is that it may be put on display *before* a decision is made. Participants are invited to supplement the elements displayed. The challenge to find some omissions in the display of the situation, for which a decision was sought, is something that very few employees can resist.

Because the decision has not been made, even tentatively, the addition of new elements simply means the addition of some new component under the appropriate parameter. It is quite unlikely that, with a good sampling of the various groups of persons to be affected by a decision, a whole new parameter will ever need to be added. But even this offers little difficulty.

### *What is a good decision?*

Not only does a "good" decision provide a workable solution to a problem, but the solution must be acceptable to those who are to be affected by it.

If management bases its decision on suggestions from a very limited number of its organization, it is very likely to be unaware of some fundamental elements in the situation for which a decision must be made.

When the ideas of a large proportion of those affected by a decision are received and incorporated, especially when the contributors can see that their ideas have been considered, the opposition to the decision is materially lessened.

The morphological display, by its constant presentation of the total problem, makes far more certain the consideration of any given element in terms of its relationships to the whole situation, and not merely in relationship to a limited area.

## 4. Respect and Utilize Your Intuitive Powers

### *Intuition and the intellect*

Utilization of the subconscious, the intuition, results in better decisions. Many of this country's greatest scientific, creative minds have told me that time and again their intellect has been completely stopped in the solving of a problem. When handed over to their intuition, further progress has always resulted.

The intellect is primarily analytical, is chiefly concerned with breaking down complex situations into ever smaller components, so that they may be observed, classified, and put to practical use.

The analytical intellect tending to move in processes of dissolution has achieved nuclear fission, but has never created anything. It takes intuition to create or to comprehend the meaning of creation.

Growing intellect often opposes instinctive wisdom, blocking its translation into creative achievement. One aspect of the intellect in particular, conscious reflection, is frequently a block between intuition and its creative expression.

Since time immemorial various procedures have been utilized to make man more sensitive to his intuitive experience. One common element in most ways of increasing sensitivity to intuition is that of freeing man from his logical intellect and his customary preoccupation with the sensory world.

According to mythology, the Delphian oracle was given drugs which paralyzed certain portions of her brain, so that she could create images that were entirely distinct from intellectual reasoning.

### *Something about the nature of intuition*

An animal, whose instinct far exceeds its reasoning power, is at the same time less intelligent but wiser than man. Birds are able to navigate for thousands of miles and arrive at the same nest which they had used the year before. Animals can find their owners who have moved great distances to new homes.

The story of man himself can not be expressed in terms of the intellect. Many intuitive experiences are involved that can not be expressed verbally.

Intuition is a primary attribute of man, one that enables him to penetrate into the heart of phenomena, while the intellect only interprets what the intuition comprehends. Intuition seeks the oneness of purpose and meaning in the relationships between a multitude of phenomena. A multitude of separate ideas may be synthesized by intuition.

Intuition, being one with the creative spirit itself is the instrument of creativity and comprehension. The creative in one person responds to the creativity in other people and in nature. This is often demonstrated by the great increase in excellence that results when one finds himself in the company of superior artists, musicians, bowlers, or athletes.

Intuition may be seen as a spiritual process wherein creative forces become aware of themselves. Intuitive perception is an absolute reality, which must be supplemented by the training of the physical senses and also by logical reasoning.

A calculating machine bears resemblance to man's intellectual activities but of course has nothing whatever that is analagous to man's intuitive factors. This is why one of the most far-reaching mistakes of present-day thinking is to believe that comprehension is the result of an intellectual effort.

### *Comprehension and creativity are fruits of intuition*

The ability to comprehend probably differs only in degree from the ability to create. A creative idea is nothing more than an attribute of ingenuity, however, until it has been given a separate existence in some medium of expression.

### *Why man needs to develop his intuition*

Modern man is said to have the least wisdom and the greatest freedom of any people who have ever lived. The farther science pushes the frontiers of knowledge, the less adequate become the materialistic foundations on which Western culture has been attempting to build.

Intuitive perception has faded in modern man, but it can, and must be reawakened if man is to remain what we call human.

Intuition and creativeness have lessened during the passage of the years, while man's analytical intellect has increased in strength. The human spirit is hard to reach in a generation which has nearly lost the faculty of intuitive experience. Modern thinking has become so shallow that it has great difficulty in either sensing or solving problems of deeper significance. If intuition were to be allowed to die fully, there is no achievement or improvement in life that could give happiness. Any person whose intuitive creative powers have been developed along with his analytical abilities will see his world and its problems in an entirely different light.

Man is seriously in need of discovering and utilizing the streams of creativeness which he has acquired and to which he adds through his experiences. At a time when man was more intuitive than he is today, when his innate powers had not been fully translated into technology, his achievements and his abilities were predominantly creative. Man's intuitive sensitivity is best awakened by disciplined meditations, such as are used in divine worship.

### *Education's responsibilities for training in intuition*

In education we give full attention to the physical and intellectual development of students, but neglect almost entirely their intuitive growth. In our schools we teach how to use physical senses on the surface of our existence, meanwhile neglecting the development of intuitive perception, of looking within. Our nation is now in grave danger. Unless we train our students in the development of their intuitive power, as we do their sensory perception and intellectual understanding, our position can become critical.

The answers which a child receives to his questions are like the food received by his body. Unfortunately, most of the answers given makes the asking of the questions a futile experience.

Every bit of information presented in our schools or in training programs in industry, should be so imparted that the student is challenged, and his imagination and creativity stimulated. Today the curse of undiluted intellectualism is encroaching on our young children, making them but caricatures of adults. The over-argumentative youngster we so commonly experience is very likely that way because he has been exposed to too much reasoning before he reaches high school. Again, too much information, of the "quiz kid," teaching-machine type may very well overwhelm a child's inner growth. When received too early, intellectual growth, in excess, blocks a youngster's intuitive growth.

What a small child has and what the grownup must revive is intuitive perception and expression. In his efforts to revive his own intuitive sensitivity, an adult can do no better than to observe in the children around him the clues to his own intuition submerged in cultural intellectuality.

Modern youth needs adventure, and much delinquency results from the fact that so much of the little adventure that is within his reach is against the law.

The searching question is being raised more and more, "How

can a teacher appeal to something that he himself has not appreciated or expressed—his intuitive power?"

## 5. Be Certain that Proposals Being Considered Refer to the Same Problem

### *A good decision implies a legitimate choice*

The great majority of arguments between two persons arise because the opponents are talking about different things. The umpire of a dispute must recognize this and bring the discussion to bear on the same problem before he can make a good decision. Much the same things take place when a decision has to be made between possible choices of action.

Unless precautions are taken, it is often found that the proposed solutions are for different problems entirely. If this differentiation is not sensed by the one deciding, he is very apt to approve the best sounding solution, rejecting others which may in reality be more closely related with the real problem under consideration.

To be certain that all participants are concerned with the same problem, it is imperative that all participants are trying to achieve the same objective. It is only when the common objective is seen by all persons involved that the problems in the way of achieving that objective can be listed, and one at a time be selected for possible solutions. Then a decision may be made in favor of the solution that best solves a given problem and conforms with any specifications that may have been set up.

Since a decision always involves a choice between two or more alternatives, it is necessary that there be available some dependable basis for a choice. The first step is to eliminate as soon as possible all "impossible" solutions or proposals.

### *Multiple problems may result in some irrelevant proposals*

It is a very effective procedure—if you suspect that all participants in a discussion are not talking about the same problem—to ask each person to state what he believes is the *other* person's problem as he has presented it. When the participants are able to agree on a single statement that involves the points of view of everybody, then their proposals can have a relevancy that makes a good decision possible.

In the heat pump decision, discussed in section 1 of this chapter, the solution of Research and Development people, who were thinking of the best type in terms of efficiency, cost and maintenance, could not be expected to be the same as that attractive to the Sales Department.

A good decision will need to consider the total effect on all persons affected by the decision. A decision, for example, relative to changing the form of a business report on the basis of the savings to the accounting department of $1,000 might be a very poor decision from the point of view of sales personnel. If the proposed change would add five minutes of sales time to each transaction in the store, the reduction in sales by existing personnel, or the additional sales personnel needed to sell as much merchandise, might easily cost many times $1,000.

The natural tendency is for each person to see a problem from his own viewpoint first, and when he, himself, is fully protected, then it is time to think about the other persons involved. One purpose of the morphological display shown in Figure 8-1 is to enable individuals to see that their problem and those of others are part of a broader common problem. If a solution to one partial problem adds to another partial problem, then some other solution is better. In terms of the greatest good for an entire organization, a solution that did not improve conditions for all persons affected by the decision can not possibly be the best one that can be found.

### *The "hidden agenda" barrier to good decisions*

Any suggestions intended to aid in the formulation of a decision will usually reflect some "hidden agenda" on somebody's part. Sometimes the person may not be fully conscious that this is true, but its danger to a good decision is still present.

No matter how "company-centered" a man may be, he is bound to stress at least a little more enthusiastically a solution that will cause him the least trouble, especially if it is a good solution though not the best one possible.

The only sure defense against "hidden agenda" is to have clearly in view, and sincerely accepted by all concerned, an objective whose achievement will be for the best interests of all.

### *Timing and good decisions*

The element of time is one that enters into decision making, whether observed and recognized or not. The decision to continue making the same model of car for another year might conceivably result in a greater income for another year. If the time for a financial crisis is *now,* this may be a good decision. But if the position of the company in the market in two or three years is more important than current income, then a change of model may very well be the better decision. In his position as top executive a man may be in possession of some "king value" that overrules general information available to the other participants in the decision making activities.

## 6. Reduce Mental Stress in the Minds of Those Affected by Your Decisions

### *Do you give or get ulcers?*

A Hollywood tycoon had just finished delivering a very violent tirade to someone on the other end of a telephone line. A friend sitting in the office commented, "You should be careful. That kind of thing will cause you to get an ulcer." The reply of the first speaker was, "I don't *get* ulcers; I GIVE them!"

Ulcer talk may serve as a sort of protection from disquieting ideas, and thus delay the inevitable crack-up due to the making of decisions on the basis of partial information. But it makes the dictator's own organization less useful, and less efficient.

### *Mental tensions demand relief*

The excessive, and the continual, frustration of the attainment of the irreducible needs of man must inevitably result in the creation of tension. Mental tensions, once set up in the mind of a person, cause him to seek for a release by the restoration of equilibrium. The means sought to gain this release may or may not be to the best interests of himself or to others.

Any decision that acts against the realization of fundamental needs must always be an inferior decision. Fundamental, or basic, needs so clearly described by Professor Maslow involve:

(1) The Physiological Needs
(2) The Safety Needs
(3) Belongingness Needs
(4) Esteem Needs

If these needs are blocked, those affected must expend effort in protecting themselves, the good of their associates being thus forced into the background.

Cutting costs by reducing wages conflicts directly with the *safety needs* of employees, and will be opposed or compensated for in some way or other. On the other hand, cost reduction by the reduction of waste, or the increase in efficiency—particularly when based on suggestions made by the employees—partially meets the need for self-esteem and recognition, making a better employee, instead of a poorer one.

There are two principal ways by which the mental stress from decisions may be reduced: (1) All participants should realize that the making of a decision is an executive function that can not be delegated; the responsibility of employees and staff is to provide the executive with all possible information, properly organized, so that he can make a good decision. (2) The executive should be highly sensitive to the personality effects that his decision would entail if put into effect.

### *The greatest asset—minds of men*

The most valuable asset, and the most difficult to replace when lost, is the brainpower and experience of an organization's personnel. It would seem, therefore, the part of wisdom to make the best possible use of the minds available.

The mental health, the intellectual efficiency, of any person depends on the extent to which he is able either to adjust to—or to change—the many demands made on him, without excessive tension on himself or his associates.

A decision should be so developed, and so implemented, as not to inhibit the development of or the expression of the various aspects of personality. If such blocking does occur, mental stresses are set up, which must result in a lowered efficiency of those affected.

Much is heard about the lack of self-confidence and the unwillingness of employees to assume responsibilities, or to attempt the solving of problems where there is a high possibility of failure. The excessive conformity demanded by professional organizations and industrial organizations alike, contributes toward a low confidence level. Conformity provides protective ruts in which to move, thus giving a false sense of security.

A *sudden* decision that tears people ruthlessly from a familiar structure, or destroys the familiar structure which they have erected about them, immediately conflicts with the basic need for security. Decisions, even good ones, that fail to offer those affected by the decision a real opportunity to participate in acquiring the data on which the decision is to be based will result in low confidence and a lack of initiative.

### *What is meant by personality?*

Personality is an aggregation of many kinds of traits. If these are well organized, the person is free from tension, and is efficient. If these traits are disorganized, a personality is under tension, and is inefficient. Each person is an unique entity, unlike any other person, and should be regarded as an individual and not simply as a part of a group.

There are many concepts and definitions of personality. Probably one of the most useful concepts of personality is that set forth by Dr. J. P. Guilford, of the Department of Psychology at the University of Southern California.

Dr. Guilford looks at the personality from seven points of view: Interests, Attitudes, Temperament, Needs, Physiology (organic functions), Morphology (structure) and Aptitudes (Abilities to perform).

***Some good and bad decisions***

In any of the *Areas of Life* and *Problem Systems,* discussed in Chapters 2 and 8, will be found situations which may, at the discretion of the decider, either increase or decrease the mental stress in the minds of those affected by the decision.

Let us consider education in the community. One very common problem of widespread concern, is that of cheating in examinations. The standard decision is to watch the students very carefully during examinations, and to warn a student the first time he is caught, to fail him in the examination the second time, and to expel him from the course for the third offense.

Another decision that might be made would be to so modify the examinations that the normal desire to cooperate with one another by the sharing of ideas is encouraged. The examination to be so framed that the individual's ability to *use* ideas would be amply demonstrated.

Again, let us look at a discipline problem on the job. An employee starts coming in five or ten minutes late each morning. Decision 1: Dock the man more and more each time that he is late until he starts arriving at work on time. Decision 2: Find out *why* the man is late, assuming that he is not at fault until so proven. Should it be found that the man's wife and children are sick, and that his daily housekeeper has great difficulty in arriving at the man's home so that he can leave home early enough in the morning to be at work in time, give the man an hour off at the beginning of the day until his wife is up. It is most unlikely that the man so treated would let this consideration cost his company anything. It would probably pay very good dividends.

## 7. Reduce False Values

***A true value of yesterday may be a false value today***

The passage of time often makes values that were entirely legitimate turn into false values. Fifty years ago an investment in an up-to-date livery stable would have been considered a wise decision. The same decision today would, in most instances, be in terms of a false value.

When the *actual* values being sought are not worth the risks involved, the decision is not a good one to make. The evaluation of a decision is greatly facilitated if you will search for the values being stressed in reality. Most adults make their personal decisions regarding their behavior, their religion, their politics, on the basis of events and influences experienced during their teens or earlier.

### *False values in the home*

The school nurse in a neighboring community had occasion to visit an underprivileged home to find out why the children were not attending school. Over the noise of a new television set, and in between answering calls on a colored princess telephone set, the mother explained that the children had no shoes and there was no money with which to buy new ones. A television and a princess telephone are both appropriate in themselves but in this case were certainly false values, so far as the health and the education of the children were concerned.

Family discipline is full of false values affecting decisions. One of the most frequently observed false values utilized, when other values have been lost sight of is, "You do this, because I say so!" The appropriate *true value* would be reasonable cooperation in the attainment of a common objective, the use of attraction of a desirable goal in place of the threat of an undesirable result.

Many thousands of decisions regarding purchases are made daily on the basis of advertising. Automobiles are sold on "snob" appeal. Hair preparations are offered with the promise that the user will have to run away from the girls if he uses two dabs instead of one.

A false value cannot be judged solely in terms of itself. Large fins on your car are a necessity if you are attempting to break the world's land speed record for automobiles, but are of absolutely no stabilizing value if you are driving your car on the public highway at any legal speed.

The actual purpose of a car is to provide safe, comfortable, and economical transportation. A true value. Enormous fins and truck horsepower are false values that must be reduced if good decisions are to be made in the selection of a new car.

### *False values in business*

A prominent sales manager told me, in all seriousness, that it was absolutely necessary for any salesman who aspired for promotion to sales manager to have satisfactorily demonstrated his ability to drink freely and to hold his liquor. Is the ability to drink hard liquor a true or a false value to the user of the merchandise or the services?

In the selection of employees for promotion, false values are in too many instances determiners. Membership in the country club is deemed of more importance than evidence at hand of achievement that demonstrates true ability and value to an organization.

### *False values in education*

In one extensive study, 80 per cent of the high school students in the lowest quarter of scholastic achievement had cars of their own. In the same study it was found that but 10 per cent of the students receiving grades that put them in the top quarter of their classes owned their own cars.

The students themselves made the decision to own their own cars. For the most part, notwithstanding the financial strain of maintaining a car, the students wanted them because of the "rate" it afforded them. The esteem of others is a basic need and quite legitimate, but in the light of car ownership, effect on high school grades and preparation for life, it must be considered a false value—to be reduced if at all possible.

A certain star-studded West Coast football team was being knocked around by greatly inferior teams to the puzzlement of the fans and the coaching staff. Eventually, it was observed that when an Eta Bita Pi fraternity member halfback was handed the ball by the quarterback, the Tappa Kega Beer blockers and linemen would somehow fail to open the holes needed for a gain. The false value—in the football game—of the glory of Tappa Kega Beer fraternity was one of the most false values the players of that fraternity could have sought.

# 9

## HOW TO SOLVE PROBLEMS

### *The nature of a problem*

A problem has an infinite number of solutions, no one of which is ever right or wrong. A question may receive an answer that is either right or wrong.

How many persons are there in a room?—is a question that has but one correct answer, at any given time. How to protect the personnel around a nuclear reactor is a problem that has an unlimited number of possible solutions, with the relative desirability of the solutions changing with existing conditions.

Problems may be entirely in the blue, that is they may be outside the experience of any person, in the form of a challenge of the unknown.

The broad technical interests of a large company, such as the General Electric Company, provides it with a great variety of challenging problems. Some of the problems may be directly related to company business, such as how to improve the efficiency of a transformer, or how to reduce the cost of a washing machine in order to meet competition.

Sometimes problems are sought in order to utilize some very promising solution that has been uncovered in basic research. Dr. J. W. Coltman, of Westinghouse Research Laboratories, noted some unusual facts about secondary emission of electrons which later proved to be the solution of the X-ray amplifier.

## 1. Develop Problem Sensitivity

### *Develop a clear picture of the ideal*

A very clear picture of what is right, established in the subconscious, is the simplest way to become sensitive to a problem that has arisen in any area.

The development of an ideal for an institution demands, first, a consciousness of its real purpose; and second, the recognition of the basic objective; and third, a knowledge of the problems that are in the way of progress toward that objective.

While the guiding image is largely intuitive, the intellectual activities associated with the acquisition and the organization of knowledge gained by response to sensory stimuli must not be overlooked, if a dependable image is to be produced. The holding of these images while solving a problem provides guidance and increased sensitivity.

The kind of images that an individual has in mind while he is in problem situations are highly significant in the questions that come to mind. George Westinghouse, when he was held up by a rear end collision between two freight trains, sensed the possibilities of replacing handbrakes that were applied on one car after the other, by air brakes that were effective on all wheels on all cars, instantly.

### *Finding hidden problems*

The Penney store manager said, "I look in drawers and files for 'problems' that have been hidden there. It is often easier to put something out of sight than to care for the conditions that may have been responsible."

Sensitivity to problems involves familiarity with the specifications of the problems. Much difficulty in problem solving results from the practice of attempting to find a solution before the specific requirements are understood. Writing down all specifications of a problem prior to trying to solve it saves much waste of time and effort.

### *The beginning of a problem*

A problem begins in a state of hopeful confusion. Without faith in your ultimate success the problem becomes a frustration. A situation is not a problem until you allow it to become perplexing.

In bringing meaning to the general chaotic beginnings of a problem, first search for the attributes and the independent variables, then for the basic relationships between them, and finally for a generic statement of the problem and then a specific statement. Solving a problem is much like the writing of a poem. Both begin with a feeling of inadequacy. This is part of the preparation stage in problem solving.

### *Problem solving is creativity*

Creativity is the basic ingredient of solving original problems. Since each one has within him the seed of unlimited creativity, if one is conscious of a problem to solve he also has within him solutions and the means of achieving them.

Problem sensitivity is a prime requisite of the creative person. It is closely associated with a questioning attitude.

Creativity begins in a state of confusion, in which a promise of something is felt. Creativity begins with a dim cloud of an idea which must be condensed into a rainfall of words. Creativity begins with a vague feeling of confused excitement accompanied by a strong feeling of an approaching, or potential, resolution of the problem.

The poet John Dryden in *Dedication of the Rival Ladies* said, "In that first tumult of my thoughts, there appeared a disorderly kind of beauty which gave me hope that something worthy might be drawn from them."

Problem solving, like creativity, involves the theory of games, the laws of chance. Straight logical reasoning is not all, nor even most, of the creative process.

### *The determiners of problem sensitivity*

"Problem sensitivity means that ability which makes men sensitive to their surroundings," according to Dr. J. J. Guilford of the University of Southern California. Carl Rogers and Ross Mooney talk about "openness to experience," the awareness that a problem exists—a hunch.

The awareness of a problem is only a feeling that one has. It is very hard to define. I start out, in approaching a problem, by listing my feeling that something is wrong. Then I continue with an "organized" random attack on my nebulous feeling.

To solve a problem one needs to be really disturbed about it. To become disturbed about a problem, just listen to what the problem is saying. Professor Jay A. Young of King's College in Pennsylvania, claims that, "Trouble in sensing problems comes from a consciousness of too many difficulties."

Problem sensitivity helps us to see the differences that exist.

## 2. Approach Problems with Confidence

### *If you can understand a problem—you can solve it*

If a problem *ought* to be solved, it *can* be solved. If a problem *can* be solved, *you* can solve it.

The highly creative person loves to solve problems. Not necessarily to find specific answers to specific questions. The creative person is stimulated by a difficulty.

### *Approaching a problem*

The concept of problem approach means the organization of one's thinking for the systematic solution of problems. Methods of problem approach have been developed through a continual study of creative people and their methods of accomplishment. One sure way of selecting creative persons is to observe how they respond to a problem around them, especially if it is not their direct responsibility.

### *A clear objective establishes confidence*

A clear objective serves in a problem-solving situation as does a ship's compass to the pilot. If an error is made in either case, it soon becomes apparent and may be corrected promptly. In problem solving, as in navigating a vessel, see what has to be done and have the nerve to do it. From time to time one should challenge himself by a statement of the beliefs on which he is acting. In experimental design one frequently asks what am I trying to do—what errors are permitted?

### *Confidence through failure*

The creative person is disturbed about problems for which he may not have any responsibility, and has the courage to do what has to be done. The creative person realizes that progress is made through failure, as well as through success. The creative individual is willing to "stick his neck out!" Being willing to "stick one's neck out" develops the intensity of interest and self confidence that is necessary if he is to rise above the average.

The ability to learn through failure has accounted for most of our great inventions and scientific advances. William Mason left the heat and pressure on in an experimental press when he was out to lunch. When he returned he found the first sheet of Masonite. Charles Kettering broke his arm while cranking a car with his right hand—and invented the self-starter.

The willingness to gamble, to take a chance, plus the energy to carry a new idea through to tangible results, is the very basic requirement of the creative personality. The creative person has to be daring, to be a leader in his group. He must constantly take calculated risks as he attempts to find better solutions for the problems facing mankind. Willingness to gamble, to take a chance, is another form of initiative.

### *How to approach vague problems with confidence*

If you will constantly try problems that are beyond what you have previously done, your frequent success will encourage you to try still other problems. Every person has at his command a tremendous amount of data which, if handled with confidence as well as with competence, will allow him to solve many problems that he normally would not consider himself qualified to handle.

To be certain that one is beginning to solve a problem properly, first study the problem *qualitatively*. Think up all possible phases of the problem, acquire a detailed knowledge of the problem, and then study the trends of the situation, including the relationships between the parts of the problem.

The first step in the solution of a problem is to gather and to organize all the known facts about the problem. In order to get all of the facts from all persons the giving of information must be a pleasant experience. This is the reason why it is so vital in all forms of idea collecting to refrain completely from evaluating ideas as they are being gathered. This is true in brainstorm sessions or in the anonymous method using unsigned cards, as in morphological creativity.

Imagination is highly important in the idea collecting period that occurs early in problem solving. Many of the finest ideas come from the subconscious and at the time can not be consciously substantiated. These ideas will not usually be offered if the identity of the source is known, hence the use of anonymity is appropriate.

### 3. Determine the Real Problem to be Solved

***A very clever solution may be a very poor one***

In many cases it is discovered that the real problem is considerably different from the one that was originally accepted as the one to be solved. It does a commuter very little good if he sprints down the station platform and catches the train for Washington, D. C. when he is actually bound for New York.

Jet pilots were assumed to fly by accelerometer. It was discovered that they actually flew by the horizon. It is of critical importance that one should be sure that he is talking about the real problem in a situation. The real problem may not be how to build a better mousetrap, but how to get rid of the mice. This latter is what is called an "open-ended" statement of the problem. It is better than a more specific statement, such as a better mousetrap, as the possible solutions are then without limit and if the mice are eliminated the need for traps has been eliminated.

At present men and machines are being seen as integral parts of a comprehensive system. The combination of both makes the solution of problems more economical and efficient.

In evaluating solutions the fundamental references should always be considered. In the Sperry artificial horizon, for example, the instrument's horizon tips in one direction but the plane has to be tipped in the other direction to bring it back into position.

### *How to define a problem*

The great need in problem solving is to define the problem. A problem well stated is almost solved. You are often advised to *start* with a clear statement of the problem. This is very bad advice. It is impossible to follow if a problem of any complexity is involved, without acting in a prejudiced manner. It is also unwise to attempt to define the problem even as basically as your initial understanding permits. If you do define the problem on the basis of anything but as complete knowledge as you can possibly obtain, you will have a concept or image by which you will evaluate subsequently submitted ideas. This is why the open-ended problem statements are best.

### *The four categories of problems*

Industry, in particular, is concerned with four types of problems, depending on whether they are: (1) specific, (2) general, (3) of immediate need, (4) of long range need.

### *The real problem can be found by synthesis only—not by analysis*

The smaller the size of the parts into which a machine, a book, or a problem is divided, the less becomes the meaning of the individual part. For example, the individual letters of the alphabet have little meaning when considered individually. It is the relationship of letters as they form words, as words are organized into sentences, sentences into paragraphs, paragraphs into chapters and chapters into a whole book that gives the individual letters their real significance.

We are advised to break down the job, to question every detail, to develop a new method, and then to apply the new method. If you are simply attempting to make a slight improvement in the same basic solution of a familiar problem, this advice may be followed without disaster. However, if you are attempting to find the best solution to a new problem, this advice is bad.

An unprejudiced approach to a new and vague problem will begin with a sense that something is not as it should be. The very next step should be the acquisition of as much information as can possibly be acquired. When all of this information has been synthesized into the real problem, then this real and total problem may be analyzed into its fundamental parts for effective treatment by appropriately qualified people.

After the legitimate analysis of the synthesized problem, the sub-problems are then listed in terms of their immediacy and suitability for attack. The relative importance of the problem elements will also serve as a guide to action. It is obviously more worth while to make a 25 per cent improvement in a very important phase of the problem than a 50 per cent improvement in some very minor phase. Recognize those areas of a problem where maximum gains are possible.

Remember, a complex problem may be seen as a total problem, only if a systematic synthesis of the known elements precedes any attempt at analysis.

### *How to analyze an established problem*

A Protestant girl who was married to a Jew immediately began to solve her problem of marital conflict when she faced the basic question, "Shall our children be Jews?" When a person does not learn what the real problems are, he is relegated to a place near the bottom of the problem solvers.

### *There are always simple solutions to the real problem*

Simplification will produce a better solution. An automatic transmission has 1,850 parts, just to shift gears. There certainly must be some better way, one that does not absorb from 10 to

15 horsepower, to accomplish what one can do with a stick moved by one finger.

The more fundamental the approach, the simpler the solution. As the solution brings together more and more of the fundamentals, it is becoming a better solution. Structuring toward simplicity and basic unity of all problem elements should be the objective of all creative problem solving.

### *How to use the problem fundamentals*

A fundamental is that *element* which gives a greater understanding of a problem. If too large or too small elements are used, loss of understanding results. Consideration of the fundamentals is a dynamic in the development of problem solving.

The consideration of problem fundamentals uncovers the basic principle that is involved in any situation. According to his associates, Mr. George Romney, the president of the American Motors Company, derives his strength and his assurance from his unwavering search for the *principle* involved, in any problem or argument.

While the arranging of the fundamentals of a problem in terms of their relative importance is helpful in the apportioning of time and effort to be spent on the problem, it should never be forgotten that premature isolation of the fundamentals of a problem is to be avoided. First should come the acquisition and organization of all available data into the real problem, not the assumed problem.

### *How to visualize complex problems*

To gain the total perspective of a problem, the problem should be considered as part of a larger system. To appreciate the meaning of a problem means to be sensitive to the existence of some more basic problem. The development of insight results from seeing the parts of a problem in terms of the total problem and the problem being solved as part of a greater problem.

Everything we do, or are, or become, is synchronous within the "total" system. As you see clearly where you are headed, and how your specific tasks contribute to a larger, more inclusive whole, you will be more highly motivated, and usually much more successful.

## 4. Produce Multiple Solutions

### *A problem has no answer*

An answer is a reply to a question. A solution to a problem is a response to a whole situation, and involves an explanation. Solutions to creative problems form an endless spectrum. There is always a better or a worse solution than any that exist at any given time in the spectrum.

Creative problems always have more than one appropriate solution. There is no one right answer to a creative problem. The practice of medicine, for example, is a continuous challenge to imagination. In making diagnoses a physician must conceive all possible alternatives in the treatment of the trouble.

### *Multiple solutions in problem solving*

The current emphasis in creativity reflects the ever widening demand for new and better solutions to both old and new problems. A new formalism, a new mental concept, results from a many-sided study of a problem. At M.I.T. when the students of Professor John Arnold's creative engineering classes were required to turn in two or more solutions to a problem, instead of simply one good one, a marked increase in the quality of the accepted solution resulted.

It is characteristic of a creative person to insist on having several solutions to a problem. Most successful computer programmers define objectives to be attained and consider many solutions. The composite solution should be close to the optimum.

### *Avoid frustration with multiple solutions*

One way to avoid frustration is to have so many things to do, so many problems to solve, that while you are incubating one or more, you are going ahead positively on others. Our failure to think up enough alternatives is the answer to the frequent question, "Why, oh why, didn't **I** think of that?"

***You can't choose the best solution from one solution***

Unless one has attacked a particular problem from six or seven directions he can have no basis for defending the solution that he proposes as being the best one available.

A highly talented research inventor in electronics said, "I ask my men, 'Why work so hard against a block—look for a door in the wall.' " The same scientist also tells his men, "Don't spend so much time on *this* solution. Try some others."

Insist on having several solutions to a problem.

A solution involves both the problem and the solver. Every design is a compromise achieving the best solution within a given time. Alternate solutions are set down for each of the unsolved phases of a problem.

A consideration of cost and time will always simplify and improve solutions.

***The evaluation of partial solutions***

In seeking better solutions to problems facing them, sometimes people are diverted momentarily by different solutions, rather than better solutions. Being able to distinguish between *better* and just *different* solutions is one mark of a truly creative problem solver.

Sometimes the need will be outlined in advance and a specific solution within restricted specifications sought—a solution that will simply fill the need adequately. The best solution can be arrived at if the implied needs of man can be given the same consideration at the same time that the more direct expressed need is being investigated. The industrial stylist and the human engineer are examples of what I mean.

## 5. Utilize Progressive Intuition

***Free your intuition from intellectual blocks***

We have now apparently reached the frontier of intellectual power. Any great progress in the future will come as the result of the development and the release of man's intuitive powers.

As the result of scores of interviews with scientists, writers, composers and artists, I am quite certain that no significant discovery has ever come solely as the result of conscious mental activity. Time after time I was told of the successful solution of some problem being achieved only after it had been released to the subconscious, or intuition.

Claude M. Bristol and Harold Sherman, in their great book, *T.N.T. or the Power Within,* tell about the practice of Alva Edison of taking multiple cat naps as he worked on an invention. When he felt blocked, after exerting himself to the utmost, he would lie down on his couch and fall asleep. He claims to have always received some additional light on his problem.

Intuitive cognition is, of course, unreliable unless preceded by an energetic effort to gain intellectual knowledge, and unless followed by an intellectual evaluation of the results of applying the intuitively derived idea.

The true solutions of our intellectual problems rest in the subconscious intuition. But your conscious, intellectual mind is incapable of understanding, of interpreting, or of evaluating many intuitive ideas directly. Many great ideas are lost because of an intellectual failure to appreciate them. Your inner mind, with its vast store of accumulated knowledge—plus that to which it has access—is aware of conditions to which your conscious mind is completely insensitive.

External perception is largely intellectual, and learned. Internal perception is intuitive, is developed within. To regain use of the submerged intuitive power which man commonly demonstrated in early times—and which is now largely restricted to so-called uncivilized people, children, elderly folks, and those called artistic—practice listening to and following the suggestions of your intuition. Verify from time to time, by standard intellectual procedure, the results of the application of the intuitive idea.

Practiced problem solvers who, when they arrive at the frustration stage, turn over to their subconscious mind their problem, are much more apt to arrive at an insightful solution than those who fret and fuss, who in effect react negatively rather than positively.

### *Intuitive sensitivity to problems*

The secret of tapping your intuitive power lies in two positive actions, *release* and *faith*. When the relatively limited intellectual forces of the conscious mind have done their best, and have failed, turn the problem over to your subconscious. Then see that your conscious mind keeps its "cotton-picking hands" off the problem. It is not very hard to trick your conscious mind into releasing its grasp of the problem. Your conscious mind really doesn't like to bother with the same problem for too long a time. It welcomes diversion. So direct the problem to your subconscious mind and immediately set your conscious mind at another task. This device always works and your subconscious quickly and persistently goes to work.

This matter of faith in the intuitive power of your subconscious is something that must be experienced. It can never be proved intellectually. The greater your faith in your intuitive powers, the greater will be its achievements. Try and see for yourself; it never fails.

### *Listen to the voice of your intuition*

The "voice within you" always speaks when you make up your mind what you want and then go after it. When you are undecided, worried, doubtful, or afraid, you cannot hear your inner voice. Mahatma Ghandi, who almost single-handedly brought about the release of India from Great Britain, told the British officials in England, "I am doing this because an inner voice within me speaks."

God speaks to men in their moments of greatest need. Their inner resources of creative power are tapped. Of this I can speak with the greatest assurance. It has happened to me frequently enough so that I can approach any problem facing me with calm assurance in the unlimited creative, intuitive power available to me.

As ideas float up from the depths to your conscious mind

write them down or otherwise act upon them at once. They descend as swiftly and as mysteriously as they appear. If you make a habit of missing good ideas by inaction, you will find that you will not be offered as many.

### *How to tell if your hunches are sound*

The more generally accepted word "hunch" means nothing more or less than an intuitive suggestion. Your hunches are the end products of your subconscious efforts in your behalf. Treat them just as you would any other idea.

### *How to have a settled mind*

An unsettled mind results in unsettled conditions, by attracting unsettling elements to it. A firm purpose, a clear objective, well-defined problems, and a genuine concern for others will enable you to utilize to the full your intuitive powers.

The difficulty in making decisions is usually the result of being unwilling to discard old patterns of thought that are in conflict with verified intuitive suggestions.

The *unlimited* extent of your intuitive power, when understood and trusted, will give you unlimited confidence as you seek solutions to problems. Strong decisions are the only cure for doubts.

### *Ways to stimulate your intuition*

A clear picture of the problem that you are trying to solve—either a word picture, a line drawing, or just a mental image—will always stimulate your intuitive output.

Remember to give thanks for the intuitive suggestions that you receive. It helps mightily to keep ideas coming. This you perhaps may neither understand nor believe. *Just try it for yourself.*

The intuitive "faculties" are developed mostly at times of meditation, when one is thinking of giving instead of getting.

Another *sure* way of increasing sensitivity to your inner voice is to put purpose and principle above personal needs or power. As you forget yourself your intuitive perception will become stronger. Once you have really made up your mind to do a thing, it will be done.

It is not simply to afford an added bit of comfort that psychiatrists, and research scientists like Dr. J. R. Oppenheimer, have couches in their office. Both types of individuals are dealing with the intuition, and seek every means of releasing intuitive concepts to the conscious mind. Physical relaxation always helps the intuitive mind in its mysterious activities.

True humility and creative altruism will, without fail, stimulate intuitive sensitivity and intuitive productivity.

### *The synthesis of intuition*

An army, a team, or even a mob, is not an aggregation of individuals—but a synthesis of intuitive power.

Skillful lawyers fuse the intuitive minds of the jury to gain the decision desired. The facts of the case are often of relatively little importance in influencing the jury. It make take more intellectual ability than the jury possesses to appreciate technical facts fully, but they will often follow their intuition in arriving at a verdict.

William J. J. Gordon, formerly of the Arthur D. Little Company in Cambridge, Massachusetts, is probably one of the greatest exponents in this country of the art of the psycho-synthesis of the intuition of individuals into a group intuition. This "synthesized group intuition" is capable of creative achievements that are far beyond that of any individual in the group or the total combination of their separate efforts.

Portuguese Men-of-War, better known as jellyfish, can be put through a fine screen and the small pieces will regroup themselves once again into a complete functioning jellyfish. The separate pieces assume functions different from those in the original jellyfish.

## 6. Display the Total Solution for the Real Problem

### *The evaluation of solutions*

It is impossible to evaluate a single object, or a single idea at a time. When it seems as though we are conducting solo evaluation, we are actually considering two things—one real, tangible; and one fabricated out of the sum total of our past experiences.

In problem solving think up all possible solutions and ways of testing them. Then select the most appropriate one to test.

The total problem display asks many questions relative to the problem. The solution display will have a similar structure, consisting of answers to the questions asked by the problem display. Once the total problem has been displayed, you then have a pattern by which to evaluate the total solution. If some essentials of the total problem have been neglected, then the solution is incomplete. Refer back to the heat pump problem in Chapter 8.

Before the results of the creative individual's labors are communicated to others, he tests his creative achievement on himself. He looks at his work as if he were someone else, apart from himself, and with whom he is communicating.

The availability of a total problem display makes possible the detached evaluation of partial or total solutions. Really good writers have the ability of standing a little way back, and of observing themselves at work, as they work. A professional writer develops the ability to be someone else, other than himself.

Sometimes illumination will supply unsatisfactory solutions, if some vital fact has been overlooked. Thus the solution obtained will not fit the real problem. The evaluation of the proposed solutions will show the need for redefining the problem, and then finding still other solutions.

The "comprehensive designer" must investigate all possible approaches to a problem before he starts to evaluate the solutions obtained. In his creative design classes Dr. John Arnold finds that better quality of achievement results with the judgment being made by the student himself.

### *Premature evaluation will limit completeness of final solution*

Decisions are made: (1) on your own and other's experience, (2) by thinking through a problem after organizing all facts and alternatives.

If an attempt is made by the members of a group, as is so frequently done, to evaluate a partial solution in terms of itself—instead of in terms of the total solution of the total problem—a prejudiced solution only is very likely to result. Evaluation must be restrained, temporarily, while one is thinking up ideas or hypotheses.

While evaluation will inhibit creativity if it occurs too early, it plays a critical role in later states of problem solving, and must be thoroughly made.

One of the most vital steps in problem solving is the evaluation of solutions in a pilot problem, before applying the solutions to the broad problem under attack. A certain high cost automobile manufacturer did not fully evaluate its automatic transmission before public sale. 36,000 of the transmissions had to be replaced, at company expense.

Another facet of evaluation is to establish the certainty that the right solution is not being applied to the wrong problem. This requires a careful review of all specifications for the problem and the solutions.

### *The effect of strain on the evaluation of solutions*

Evaluation is best conducted in an atmosphere that is as free from strain as possible. Evaluation occurs in informal as well as in formal situations, often more effectively and easily.

### *The limits governing solutions*

Determine what limits are inherent in the solution of any problem. In the design of oil well fishing tools, that are required to go five or ten thousand feet down in a well and to pick up all kinds of objects, it must be remembered that there are only four possible motions that may be applied. The fishing tool may be raised, lowered, given a right turn or a left turn. A whole series of actions of the fishing tool can be made to occur with but these four motions.

It is often necessary to accept limitations, and to live with them until the state of the art has been developed further. The design of a miniature transmitter to fit in a fountain pen was impossible until the stages of electronic art had advanced far enough to have produced the transistor.

### *Finding problems to fit solutions*

Basic research turns up a great many unique and fascinating solutions. The researcher is intrigued by their elegance until somebody raises the question, "What is this good for?"

Such a question often proves very embarrassing, for often it can not be immediately answered, sometimes for a considerable period of time. As Dr. Coltman at the Westinghouse Research Laboratories told me, "Sometimes a solution will be had first, and an application in a problem sought . . . we have learned to be patient in such instances, for many of our most profitable inventions came about in just this order."

### *The economics involved is an essential part of solutions*

It is a rare employee who can envision his firm's need for economy. The selection of the best solution for any problem can not be made without a consideration of the economics involved.

## 7. Be Familiar with the Basic Steps in Morphological Problem Solving

### *An introduction to morphological problem solving*

The interrelationships between creativity and morphology are so intimate, and so diffused, and there are so many common elements, that any attempt to separate them is as outdated as an attempt to separate matter and energy in a nuclear age.

The first step in morphological problem solving is to assume the attributes of a morphologist. It is hoped that our readers will be willing to think like morphologists, through an understanding of the basic principles of morphology, and the ways by which morphology generates creativity. (See morphological chart of *Morphology* in Appendix.)

The catastrophic effects of the *assumed* problem approach in education, research, business, labor-management relations, and in international affairs is quite obvious.

The morphological method is a necessity in the solution of complex or initially vague problems. War and peace, smog, taxes, education, transportation, marriage, etc., are examples.

The morphologist is possessed of an inner certainty that there is hardly any problem that he can not handle.

### *Acknowledgement to Dr. F. Zwicky*

Grateful acknowledgement is made to Dr. F. Zwicky of the California Institute of Technology for the wealth of morphological material which he so generously made available to me. To our personal conferences, his letters, books, reports and his book *Morphological Astronomy* I owe my concept of morphology. *Morphological Astronomy* demonstrates the powerful effects of morphology in a highly complex field. An English translation of Dr. Zwicky's *Morphological Research,* at present in German, is now under way.

Dr. Zwicky also has in preparation a six-volume set of the applications of morphology to several specialized technical fields. This morphological work should be of very great service in helping the United States of America regain its once dominant leadership in technology and to make the necessary theoretical progress that is basic to technological status.

### *The basic principles of the morphological method*

I. Any concept resulting from a finite statement is incomplete.
II. The total knowledge to be had is always without limit.
III. Total knowledge is always sought in any field of operation.
IV. The total solution of a given problem is achieved through a knowledge of all known elements in all possible relationships.
V. There is an universal relationship between all things.

VI. Synthesis must always precede analysis, if unprejudiced decisions are to be made.

VII. A morphological structure of values sought precedes the the judging of any idea offered or solution proposed.

### *How morphology generates creativity*

I. Improves individual and group efficiency.

II. Offers freedom from internal and external barriers to creative thinking.

III. Suggests solutions to any problem.

IV. Stimulates greater independence and versatility.

V. Provides the step from intuition to systematization.

VI. Provides a dependable guide to the naming of decisions.

VII. Provides a creative symbol of the activities essential to the survival of mankind.

### *Morphological problem solving begins with synthesis, not analysis*

The identification of the problem is not the first step in problem solving. First must come the gathering of the sub-elements from all possible sources. Then the combining of these sub-elements into larger and larger components, finally becoming a dynamic structure, as shown for the heat pump in Chapter 8.

Write down all you know or can find out about a problem, just as if you were trying to convince someone that there was a problem to solve. Also write down all of the specifications for the problem—do not attempt to carry them in your head.

A complete discussion of morphological problem solving would require a large book in itself. It is hoped that the reader will, by following the detailed simple steps set forth, be able to test for himself the advantages of morphological problem solving.

Students in my classes in applied creativity at the University of Southern California, and in my private classes, have been able to follow the instructions and solve some difficult problems in business expansion, in personnel, and in production.

***The basic steps in morphological problem solving***

Step 1: Get the feel of the general problem area. Read all available material concerning the problem, marking or otherwise identifying all ideas that appear to be of any possible significance —*without any immediate evaluation.* Talk with as many people as possible who are parts of the problem in any way. Take careful notes.

Step 2: Type all of the ideas collected in step one on 2.5 by 3 inch cards, with the three inch side horizontal.

Step 3: Lay the cards on a table in blocks of twelve—three cards wide and four cards high. Leave about one quarter of an inch between individual cards, and one inch between blocks of cards. This arrangement has worked out to be the best of the many different plans that I have tried.

Step 4: Read the cards over four or five times, as quickly as you can. *All* of the ideas presented *will be retained* in your mind permanently, most of them in your subconscious. We shall make intuitive use of these "submerged" ideas during the process of setting up the total problem.

Step 5: Go away from the cards for at least half an hour, taking great pains to occupy your conscious mind so completely that it will not be thinking about the cards. Your subconscious mind will continue to work diligently on the problem, and with much higher efficiency than it could if your conscious mind simultaneously is criticizing every new idea proposed by your intuition.

Step 6: Return to the cards and again study them. You will now notice that certain of the cards appear to be friendly to one another—just friendly—and may easily be collected into congenial groups. If you had started with 500 cards you might wind up with from 20 to 30 of these friendly groups. Now write a descriptive title card for each group (use a distinctive color) and place a rubber band around the group.

Step 7: Treating each of the groups of cards now as a single element, continue synthesizing the groups into a still smaller number of groups until you finally come to no more than seven groups. Again write a descriptive card for each of these final groups. These are the fundamental elements of the problem, which are commonly called parameters. This number seven was not an arbitrary assumption, but is in recognition of the proven psychological fact that seven elements is the maximum that the human mind can consider efficiently at one time in a single group.

Step 8: Analyze the cards of each parameter into not more than seven sub-groups, called components. The original groupings as found in step six will often turn out to be components, but sometimes other arrangements will appear more suitable.

Step 9: Type the parameters, and their components, in columns, as was done in Chapter 8.

Step 10: Cut the pages up into strips of one parameter each. Then paste the strips on pieces of thin cardboard of the same size as the paper strips. Make a simple device to hold the slides. You are now ready to take a look at the real, the total, problem.

Suppose that you wind up with seven parameters, each with seven components. If each parameter slide were to be placed in all possible vertical positions, you would have more than 250,000 possible relationships indicated, all of which have a part in the total problem. This huge number will be brought down to a reasonable number by consideration of the "king value," as discussed in Chapter 4, Section 5.

A creative atmosphere is one in which every person feels free to express himself, with no fear of reprisal or ridicule. There must be some opportunities to fail. Problems should be assigned —large and small—that so far have never been solved. A challenge to try, with an understanding of possible failure recognized, is inherent in creative growth.

A creative atmosphere has a feeling of flexibility. No idea is ever rejected solely because, if accepted, it would conflict with long established practices. It requires but a very few rebuffs to dry up the fountain of creative ideas of any group.

### *Group reactions to the working atmosphere*

Although a creative atmosphere is impossible without the leadership of the supervisor, it is equally impossible of attainment without the understanding and the cooperation of the group.

A creative atmosphere will be characterized by full four-way communication. The communication must be free and complete back and forth between members of the group and up and down between the supervisor and his group.

While the element of friendly competition, in the attainment of the common objective of the group, is very desirable, there should exist, at least periodically, a relative freedom from stress if maximum creativity is to be expressed.

High pay alone will not keep an employee happy or creative. He must be able to appreciate how his particular job is essential to the attainment of the company objective. His worth as a person must be acknowledged.

The proposer of an intuitive idea is often unable to justify himself in a rough and tumble battle. He may lack the technical knowledge, or the vocabulary, to express himself, yet outstanding ideas will often come from employees who are sensitive to problems and have the desire to help solve them.

When a person expresses a new idea he is extremely vulnerable to attack. He is especially sensitive if his idea is intuitive, as are all really original ones. Unless a sensitive person feels protected, he will usually refuse, voluntarily, to expose himself.

Finally, if the working atmosphere is to be truly creative, it is necessary for the supervisor himself to be open to new ideas in his own activities in supervision.

## 2. Develop Sensitivity to Change

### *Preparation for change*

Even very simple changes, whose values may be clearly appreciated, are apt to be fought bitterly if they are not presented properly. Proper presentation includes the technical and the psychological preparation of those affected by the proposed change. A general agreement that some need is not being met adequately should precede any presentation of a proposed change in procedures.

To develop flexibility to change, an employee must have confidence that the change is not going to harm him, or to make his job any more difficult. Flexibility to change may be encouraged by lessening resistance to change, or by making changes attractive. There is some evidence that flexibility can be promoted by rewarding a person when he tries out different approaches, according to Dr. J. P. Guilford.

Strong resistance to change often results when the technology of the change is so greatly in mind that the psychological and the social effects on the employee are overlooked.

### *What employees fear in change*

The strongly self-confident person welcomes change in his job. It is the closest thing to adventure that he will find on his job. Change is the antidote to conformity which seems to be becoming increasingly prominent in our working lives today.

There seems to be little doubt that the greatest reason for the usual resistance to change is fear. Fear of the unknown. With the advent of a change, the individual's sense of personal security is gone. He is now obliged to ask, instead of confidently telling. A man who is regarded as an expert in existing procedures may find himself a novice if a change is made.

If a substantial change takes place, an employee may fear that his earnings will suffer. That he will lose status. That his chance for advancement will be impaired.

### *Some psychological aspects of resistance to change*

Psychological inertia keeps many persons working for years in a comfortable rut. It is much more comfortable not to change one's way of doing things.

As a rule, employees do not resist *technical* change, but what might be called *social* change. A change in their self-esteem and the esteem in which they are held by others. This truth is at the heart of difficulties experienced by a great many large companies who have thousands of engineers on their payroll engaged in research and development. When a piece of "hardware" is finally in a satisfactory operating condition and production begins, a serious lag often develops. Even though the need for such vast quantities of research engineers is no longer in existence, great difficulty is had in inducing these engineers to accept straightforward production responsibilities. Even though their salaries would remain the same, the drop in prestige is often a strong deterrent.

The matter of personal pride may be involved in another way, causing resistance to change. The individual resents the change primarily because he himself did not think it up, and he is unwilling for credit to go to another person.

The element of pride of "authorship" is often involved. Resistance may be expected if a change in operation would require the modification or the elimination of some procedure proposed and nurtured by an individual who is still actively involved in the operation. This is one reason why a periodic shift in personnel may be a helpful procedure.

Expecting a person to change his mind too rapidly results in mental stresses, something similar to the breaking stress in an automobile tow rope if the lead car accelerates too rapidly.

### *Participation reduces resistance to change*

Probably the most effective way to reduce, perhaps to eliminate resistance to change, is to have all persons to be affected by the change have a part in planning and implementing the change. A change that is proposed, without the participation of the employees concerned, will be taken as a personal affront to the knowledge and skill of the employees. The employees are, in effect, being told that their work has become unsatisfactory, without being made to understand that it is conditions beyond their control that demand the changes.

Simple participation in the making of changes is not enough. If not sincerely carried out this action will often boomerang. The participants must feel that their contributions are respected and valued, even though it may not be possible to incorporate all of them in the change proposed.

Resistance to change may be considerably reduced if there is an appreciation of the economic dangers that face the company if a superior procedure available is refused, and is put into effect by a competitor.

### *The supervisor's attitude*

The attitude of the men toward their supervisor will have a great deal to do with their flexibility to change. If the supervisor has built up a strong feeling of confidence in his judgment and honesty, his group will be much more willing to try out an announced change.

It is always helpful when the supervisor recognizes that employee resistance is not necessarily bad. It may be simply an indication of something that needs to be considered more fully.

Especially now that so many highly technical devices are being introduced, in competition with human efforts, it is of considerable importance that the supervisor reassure his group, that he present the new devices in terms that may be readily understood, using analogies if the theory involved is beyond his group. If the supervisor's presentation is so expressed that the basic idea can be quickly grasped, and its value appreciated, the initial resistance will be much less than if the basic idea is buried under a flood of detailed explanations.

If the supervisor is able to point out that it is the conditions that have changed, not the inherent merits of earlier suggestions, and that whatever is appropriate to the new procedure will be retained, better group feelings will result.

It is the responsibility of the supervisor to see that all persons to be affected by the proposed change be fully acquainted with the possible advantages, and that ample time is provided to become competent in the proposed procedures.

A belief that there is but one answer to any given problem, that with which the supervisor is familiar, encourages rigidity. Holding the concept that there are an unlimited number of solutions to a problem stimulates the development of a better solution than the one at present in use.

If the supervisor himself seeks change, by continually asking his men *why* they are doing a job as they are, and how it might be done more easily, or more cheaply, he will start his men to asking questions that will lead to change if answered.

## 3. Conduct Harmonious, Constructive Conferences

***The more harmony, the more ideas produced***

In this section we shall not be concerned, primarily, with the various methods by which ideas may be acquired. This has already been discussed at length in Chapter 3. Here, we shall discuss some of the ways in which a supervisor may conduct harmonious conferences.

First of all, the supervisor can always look for the *value* in all ideas, even though some may appear to be of little use. This will result in continued, hearty cooperation of group members.

Worthwhile conferences are seldom either inharmonious or dull. An harmonious conference may have many differences of opinion, but these differences are used constructively. Conferences can be so unpleasant that they are avoided whenever possible. The head of one West Coast organization so keenly resented the unpleasantness that so frequently developed in staff conferences that he flatly refused to hold them. Most disastrous results followed executive decisions based on inadequate understanding of actual conditions.

### *What is the purpose of a conference?*

There are many types of conferences, each requiring a specific approach and procedure: Policy making, objective stating, problem solving, planning, informative, morale building, attitude forming, and training—just to mention a few.

When a conference loses its specific identity with some specific problem, the conferees will become confused. An advance agenda stimulates preparation and helps to keep everybody in the group thinking about the same problem.

If creative abilities are to be developed through conferences, there must be a real challenge to the entire group. The pre-conference agenda should always answer the question, "What kind of a conference is it to be?" Then when the announced purpose of the conference has been achieved, it is a good time to adjourn the meeting.

The acceptance of a common problem is fundamental to conference harmony. The leader should restate, rephrase, recapitulate the topic to be discussed until all are in agreement as to what problem the group is discussing.

Any conference that attempts to establish objectives, to discover problems, and to find solutions at one meeting is doomed to inferior achievements.

### *A conference is not for decision making*

In group conferences there should be, of course, opportunity for the presentation of the problem situation, but in such a way that extensions of the problem will be encouraged. The supervisor should scrupulously avoid setting a fixed problem and offering a favored solution.

Although management may delegate authority to carry out a decision, and perhaps to make certain decisions, this is not a function of a group. It is of the utmost importance for a group to recognize that they are not a decision-making body, that their responsibility is to provide the ideas upon which the designated executive may make a good decision.

The *responsibility* for decisions is one that CAN NOT be

delegated. Most executives strongly resent having subordinates usurp their decision-making prerogative.

### *Most people are different*

It is quite certain that various members of any group will excel in certain particulars. But the "break-through" idea may come from the least prominent member of the group.

Personality differences may cause disruptive or divisive influences, against which the supervisor must be on guard.

Harmony may be greatly improved if the various slants and prejudices of group members are considered by the supervisor when leading his group. Disagreements may be used constructively *before* open personality conflicts occur. When the conference air begins to get a little thick it is always helpful if the supervisor will remember:

A Little Humor, Now and Then
Helps Harmony, Among all Men.

In any group of business executives there will be two major groups: (1) those who fairly froth at the mouth in their hatred of any form of group thinking, and (2) those who recognize that any group of people working together will have more knowledge and experience than any single member of the group, including the supervisor.

Some people prefer the quiet peace of solo thinking. Others enjoy the stimulation of the minds of others. The most effective groups will make use of both types.

### *Personal elements in group discussions*

The atmosphere, discussed in Section 1 of this chapter is, of course, of prime importance. Any suggestion of personal favoritism, or prejudice, quickly poisons the conference atmosphere.

Independent interests weaken a group; common interests strengthen both the group as a whole, and the members as individuals. Individual and group initiative requires reasonable freedom from restrictive control, if the potentialities are to be realized.

***Objectives, problems, and solutions***

The common tendency is to spend too much time too soon on solutions, especially when the real problem is neither clearly understood nor accepted and when there is no common objective.

Not only is the sequence of objective, problem, solution, most important to observe, but also each phase should be the subject of separate conferences, separated by appropriate time intervals.

For many of the situations facing a supervisor's group, a simple "brainstorm" session, following the established rules set up by Alex Osborn in his book *Applied Imagination,* will be helpful and economical of time.

When the problem is complex, or when personalities are involved, the anonymity of the contributor of an idea must be respected. Sometimes suggestion boxes are useful, but the writing of ideas on small cards, unsigned, as the whole group is working together is much more effective.

Whether there are 6 or 160 people in a conference, if they are seated in groups of six, at separate tables, far greater freedom of expression and greater ease are possible, than when they are formally seated in rows.

The length of conference periods will vary with the importance of the problem and the attitude of management toward the participation of employees in the solving of their own problems.

Let us say that the sub-objective under consideration by a supervisor and his group is to improve the efficiency of an automobile fuel pump. The group knows that if the pump is not improved, even more business will be lost to a competitor, and that some of the group may lose their jobs. There can be no serious objection raised by any member of the group to the objective of improving the efficiency of the fuel pump. Conference harmony can be maintained if the supervisor next asks for general answers to the question, "What are some of the problems in the way of achieving our objective, as you see it from your various viewpoints?"

If the machinist says that it is extremely difficult, with the type of metal used, to work within the prescribed tolerances, or if the installer says that it takes two men to install it because of the mount design, there is no cause for argument. Each man has stated an indisputable fact, involving a problem that needs to be solved. Of course the poor quality may be due to lack of concern on some individual's part. The men in the group realize this, but dislike to mention it openly, even though their jobs may be at stake. Here again is the place to use anonymous submission of ideas.

The synthesis of the ideas expressed should by no means be attempted by the group in conference. This is a task that is best done by the supervisor himself.

Each person has had the opportunity of contributing to the solution of the problem. He had been given a sense of freedom in the midst of the basic conformity of his job. Management will be more receptive to the group's solution because of the unity and harmony demonstrated.

## 4. Avoid the Effects of Isolated Specialization

### *The role of the supervisor*

In each supervisory group are many types of abilities and interests. One of the prime responsibilities of the supervisor is to weld his group into a smoothly working team. A team is not an aggregation of individuals, even though there are individuals who make up the group.

The supervisor will seek, not only to improve the technical skill, but the personal characteristics of his men and the human relationships existing between them.

### *Pros and cons on being a specialist*

The highly trained specialist is very apt to feel that he lacks freedom to take up other work. On the other hand, a specialist may be disinclined to learn enough to permit himself to be changed to another job, for fear of losing his position as a real expert in the work that he has been doing.

The high degree of specialization required today is making it increasingly difficult for the average worker to appreciate the over-all significance of his job. This loss of meaning, coming from isolated, analytical specialization, may be prevented by a periodical synthesis of ideas under the direction of the supervisor.

Continued specialization in one limited area is bound to result in eventual boredom and in inefficiency. Radical changes in technology may result in a man finding himself without a job. A man who is an expert solderer will find himself in difficulties if his firm goes over to the use of printed circuits.

Crossing over skill and experience lines will often result in far better solutions than technical specialists in a particular field would have produced.

### *Morale and group structure*

Pointing out that the responsibility that each person has to others in the group is vital in the overcoming of the tendency of people to be "own-job" centered. While the operations of each specialization may be quite unique, the functions form part of a total process that can be understood by all members of a group, even though members of the group may not be capable of appreciating the technical details of each other's jobs.

The highly skilled specialist is apt to feel that he is not really a part of the group; that he does not understand the others, nor they him.

To counteract the effects of isolated specialization, group action on a problem is essential. It is becoming more and more common for interdisciplinary groups to cooperate in the solving of a specialized problem. There is an increasing call for "inperts" to help the experts. The experts know all of the reasons why a certain problem can not be solved; the "inpert" wonders why it can not be solved in a given way, and, not knowing any good reason why, goes right ahead and solves it.

### *Boredom—the great hazard of specialization*

The good supervisor senses the attitude of boredom on the part of a member of his group, and tries vigorously to relieve it. Helping the subordinate to gain maximum experience from his present job, by modifying the duties of his present job in order to provide added responsibility, is one way.

Job rotation will give employees a broader understanding in the meaning of their own job. It will also indicate some of the additional skills and knowledge that one needs to advance himself.

#### *Status and promotion*

An employee is afraid that, by leaving the field in which he is regarded as an expert, his chances of promotion might be impaired. A familiarity with the route from his present specialized job to one of greater responsibility and salary will make it easier for an employee to move toward promotion.

Every employee can continually add zest to his job by looking for new and better ways of doing his work. This may be accomplished by the continuous asking of questions about the work, both by the employee himself and by his supervisor.

### 5. Enable the Soarer and the Plodder to Work Together

#### *The synthesis of group powers*

The synthesis of the intellectual and the intuitive powers of his group is the real responsibility of a supervisor. The technical development, and its utilization, are but contributors to the greater synthesis of minds. It is most critical that the divisive distrust, and lack of mutual appreciation, existing between the intellect and the intuition be synthesized into an harmonious working relationship.

The continued existence of this nation in today's culture, and of any organization or institution within that culture, depends on the creation of an active partnership between intellect and intuition.

The supervisor has the responsibility to synchronize the ideas of the plodder and the soarer into a structure of action that will be acceptable to both the analytical, intellectual plodder and the synthetical, intuitive soarer.

A supervisor who both knows his men as individuals and the

problems facing the group, is able to achieve fantastic results as he matches the problems of the group with the attributes of his men. The supervisor will have in his group people who are predominantly intellectual plodders and highly articulate. In addition there are the quiet, intuitive soarers.

### *Void if detached*

The plodder and the soarer represent the two worlds of man that exist in differing degrees in every person. Both are essential to our continued existence.

Let it be most clearly understood that my strong emphasis on the intuitive does not mean that I am advocating the abandoning of intellectual activity. I am simply insisting that *both* the intellect *and* the intuition are desperately needed today, and that either one is "void if detached" from the other.

The other day I watched my grandson plod along the diving board clear out to the end. There he stopped. He had complete confidence in the board's ability to hold him up. Beyond that he was uncertain, insecure, and afraid. After three or four attempts he finally *soared* off the board with a graceful splash dive. This was a new experience for him, even though countless others had done it before him.

Somebody had to take the first dive from a diving board. Some seagull had to be the first one to take a mussel up into the air and then drop it on the highway, breaking the shell.

It is not our purpose to try to explain the nature and the operation of the subconscious mind, or the power of the intuition. To be perfectly honest we are not able to. What we are attempting to do is to stress the existence of the tremendous, almost unused, power, and to suggest a few ways in which intuitive power may be produced and utilized.

The total synthesis, possible by morphological methods, brings together those two dichotomous elements, the intellect and the intuition, which are mutually supporting.

The oportunity must be given for the intellectual plodder and the intellectual soarer to participate in a friendly, relaxed climate.

When fully applied to the activities of any group or organization, morphological creativity will accomplish this.

National leaders in business, science, engineering, research, invention, and the arts, have stressed to me that many of their problems had stubbornly resisted all intellectual analytical attempts to solve. It was only when they had recourse to the services of their hidden resources, their intuition, that they were able to solve the problem.

### *Intuition and the intuitive*

It is not considered quite proper, in most circles, to cut loose from the facts at hand, and to go into intuitive orbit, just because it is fun. No reliable study has been able to show that creative ability is significantly related to intellectual ability or to academic achievement. Many studies, however, have shown the existence of negative relationships.

Creativity *may* involve deliberate, and organized, thinking but it *always* involves the intuition, the subconscious. The mind in creation, and in preparation for it, always requires some management. To progress we need pioneers who can enter fields in which they have had no experience, where, by their logical thought processes plus intuition, they can come up with successful solutions.

As Dr. Aaron Wexler of Westinghouse told me, the only people who could solve the really baffling company problems, are those troublesome individuals who insist on "trips to the moon."

There is no question but that the greatest part of our knowledge, understanding and experience is submerged, out of sight of our conscious mind. In dreams, and even when fully awake, some stimulus will cause a great quantity of ideas that had been submerged for years to rise up into our consciousness.

The understanding needed between the intellect and the intuition will never be brought about by pressure. Doubters, in either camp, will become convinced only as they see for themselves the unity of intellect and intuition demonstrated in the solution of difficult problems.

As is well known, most people are different. Some are cautiously intellectual and analytical. This type are needed as verifiers and interpreters. But we need even more the "space" men—men who have the courage, the curiosity, and the initiative to soar off into the unknown, men who will bring back interesting curios for the grounded intellectuals to fit into solutions that have the intellectuals thoroughly blocked. A person who tries to solve a complex problem solely by intellectual efforts, is like a one-eyed, color-blind person attempting to judge an exhibit of modern art.

### *The evaluation of solutions*

The evaluation of achievement will be highly questionable, if made from the viewpoint of either the intellect or the intuition. Any program must satisfy both the intellect and the intuition, if it is to be of the maximum effectiveness.

### *Signs of the times*

The times in which we now find ourselves are baffling the intellectual plodder. The new problems that are arising in droves can not be solved by existing methods, or by modifications thereof. Brave, fresh approaches to solutions are needed. The more fluid the times, the less effective the pure plodder becomes. He tries, and fails, to meet new situations with old, familiar, proven, logical procedures.

The problems of our culture used to advance, and to change by sections—as a long freight train starts up car by car. It used to be possible to care for a problem part by part. The change in the parts of a problem, and their relationships, was so slow that the pieces could be considered individually. Now, the whole problem, and the relationships of its parts must be seen in a single picture.

Today's problems are so complex, and so closely knit together, that a broad, total, synthesized, intuitive view must be had of even a complex problem, if adequate solutions are to be produced.

The rapidity with which conditions are changing, and the

highly complex problems that are developing, make the solutions of the intellectual analysts quite inadequate. In times that are relatively static, the intellectual plodder is highly respected and supported. He is comfortable and safe. He proposes very few changes that make people uncomfortable enough to arouse resentment.

## 6. Do Things the Easy Way

### *An easy job is hard work*

An easy job does not necessarily mean one that involves little effort or results. On the contrary, the opposite is usually true. By easy is meant freedom from constraint, stiffness, and apprehension—relaxed and not hard pressed.

### *An easy $70,000*

Complete assurance makes any job easy, even a complex one. Quality control, for example, is often very difficult because of so many elements involved and the almost infinite number of relationships between these elements.

The writer served as a guest lecturer at a California state college, speaking on morphological problem solving. A young graduate student in his late twenties took back some of the ideas to his job as a production control supervisor. Within the next month he was able to effect a saving of more than $70,000 by reducing the number of rejected parts. Before a year was up he had saved the company more than $250,000.

### *Freedom from apprehension*

Employees today are afraid of many things, particularly of changes which are beyond their control, such as the automation of manual operations. The supervisor can do much to lessen the apprehensions of this group if he maintains such relationships that his group will feel free to come to him when rumors arise. His relationship with management enables him to find out the truth, or, even better yet, to know ahead of time the facts from which rumors are apt to be derived.

The average employee, who does not have a well-developed urge for discovery or innovation, has very little initiative to propose any change for which he might later be singled out for criticism. Although an employee may, perhaps, carry out his normal intellectual activities while under apprehension, or other stress, his greatest source of power, his intuition, is blocked. The stress of apprehension may be lessened in many ways. One of the simplest is through the development of a realization that a group problem is not the full responsibility of any one individual.

***Freedom from mental tension***

The supervisor can do much to relieve mental tension on the part of his group, through a strong encouragement to express the urge to be creative that is inherent in all persons, even though usually inhibited. When a tension-building problem arises, or is seen by the supervisor to be imminent, he can bring his group together and calmly and frankly present it for their consideration.

There is often a conflict of ideas. A longshoreman must know that American shipping is having a hard time to maintain a place in world shipping, and that the practice is unreasonable of having a transfer company unload material on one pallet and store it in the warehouse, to be unloaded on another identical pallet before it can be hoisted on board ship. Yet he does not dare to raise his voice in public to protest.

***Freedom from excessive stress***

If we were to be completely honest, most of us would have to admit that we fail to do our best without pressure of some kind on us. We do achieve most when we have a deadline to meet. Sometimes the disapproval of our seniors if we fail to deliver will spur us to action. There is, however, an optimum amount of pressure appropriate to each individual. Of this the supervisor should be keenly aware, especially if he is seeking the fuller utilization of the intuitive powers of his group.

The supervisor also has the responsibility of seeing to it that the very willing individuals are not overloaded or exploited.

## 7. Do Things the Simple Way

### *The meaning of simplicity*

Simple means to be free from elaboration or artificiality. Not complex in respect to parts or structure. Unsophisticated.

On one occasion while I was discussing a problem-solving technic with Dr. F. Zwicky, of the California Institute of Technology, he commented on one of my suggestions, "It is not simple, and therefore cannot be the best way. *Make it simple*."

The concept of simplicity in reasoning exists in scientific theory at all times. Newton, for one, advanced it as a basic rule of reasoning when he said, "Nature is pleased with simplicity, does nothing in vain. More is vain when less will serve."

### *The way to simplicity*

A supervisor may achieve improvement in any phase of his work by the simple expedient of asking WHY, over and over again, until the *real* purpose emerges. There is nothing that can excel a sharp, clear view of a problem to encourage the presentation of simple, effective solutions.

For more than 200 years it had been the custom, in all stores, for a client to walk up to the counter, tell the clerk what was wanted, and then to wait until the clerk had accumulated the entire order. When the number of clerks and customers had grown to such proportions as to be unwieldy, some curious person asked, "Why not let the customer pick out his own goods from shelves and displays?"

No good reason could be found for not using both the customer's and the clerk's time more efficiently. Now the ratio of clerks to customers will be as low as one clerk to 50 customers.

The General Electric Company appliance division had been devoting a great deal of time and money to the design of its washing machines, in an effort to find some way of removing lint before it collected on clothes. The only satisfactory attachment was one that cost more than the washer itself. One of the design engineers, working on the lint problem, was helping his wife one evening by drying the dishes. His wife handed him in sequence (1) a small tin pie plate and (2) a collander.

"This is it!" he exclaimed. "We shall punch a lot of small holes in a pie tin, pump the washer water over the top and filter out the lint with no difficulty."

This modified "pie plate" may be seen today in all of the new General Electric washing machines.

Synthesis results in an increase in simplicity. Analysis, not preceded by synthesis, increases complexity by destroying relationships which give significance to the parts.

Newton simplified all known laws governing the motion of bodies into three simple statements that have guided the thinking of scientists for nearly 300 years.

Scientists engaged in basic research have developed so many new concepts that production engineers are having great difficulty in comunicating with them. For this reason a special group known as "technical writers" has arisen, whose task it is to translate the language and the problems of the production engineers.

### *There is always a simple way*

In the same manner that there are always better or worse solutions to any problem, so are there always simpler and more complex ways of doing things. Since the producer of a device or procedure that is working well will not be inclined to change, it is the supervisor who must constantly be raising the question of a better way of doing a job.

Ross Aiken, of Kaiser Electronics, expressed his own philosophy in this manner, "There *must* be a better way."

Doing things the simple way means not doing anything unnecessary in accomplishing an intended purpose. With a cloudy purpose, and a hazy concept of the problem being solved, it is very easy to retain excess operational procedures. A chimpanzee, who was participating in some learning experiments, happened to turn a somersault just before he picked out the proper lever to receive a bit of food. Ever afterwards, while trying to pick out the right lever he would turn a somersault before pulling it. It will surprise you to discover how many times employees will "turn somersaults" before approaching a problem.

### *It's natural to be simple*

In a study of the factors involved in art appreciation, Dr. J. P. Guilford found a liking for simplicity versus complexity. Those who may be called original preferred complex designs. Most persons preferred simple designs.

Dr. Guilford's discovery may be taken as a suggestion that an idea to be widely accepted should be presented in as simple a form as is compatable with complete and accurate understanding.

The supervisor may often serve as an effective simplifier when he presents a new and rather complicated solution to a problem as a functional structure, rather than as an operational one. The design and manufacture of printed circuits is a very complex process. The simple fact that with the printed circuits no soldering is necessary, except between components, is easily appreciated. An automobile may be explained far more effectively in terms of its major components—engine, transmission, chassis, etc.—than if each separate part were to be described individually.

### *The magic number seven*

In the process of an all-day conference with Professor Leo B. Moore, of the School of Industrial Management at the Massachusetts Institute of Technology, he suddenly stopped my presentation, and complained that he was badly confused by what I was telling him.

I had been discussing the possible reactions that an airplane pilot might have to take when all normal factors were taken into consideration. Appreciating the fact that if I had been able to confuse Professor Moore I had done a good job of confusing, I asked him why.

In the morphological display I had been discussing, I had used 17 parameters, each with their own components. Research has shown that the human mind is inefficient if it is asked to consider more than seven elements in their various relationships at any one time.

As discussed earlier in this chapter, and in Chapter 9, any number of ideas may be synthesized into seven parameters. If but one component in each of the parameters is considered at any given time, the magic number seven is respected.

* * *

In the painting of a picture the artist never actually finishes. One day he just stops painting and puts his art on display for what it may be worth. Such is the case with this book. It began 30 years ago and still is far from complete. We have just stopped writing for a while, and offer to you for your own use whatever has been created.

| CONTAINER CONSTRUCTION | METAL USED | TYPE OF BOTTOM | AUTOMATIC HEATING CONTROLS | CAPACITY (QUARTS) | POWER RATING (WATTS) |
| --- | --- | --- | --- | --- | --- |
| | | | | | |
| Pressed | Aluminum | Single Metal | Underneath Kettle | 2 | 500 |
| Cast | Stainless Steel | Double Metal | On Kettle | 3 | 850 |
| Single Wall | Copper | Solid | On Handle | 5 | 1350 |
| Double Wall With Air Space | | Double Bottom With Air Space | On Cord | 8 | 2000 |
| | | | | | |
| | | | | | |
| | | | | | |
| | | | | | |

**Fig. 5-1**

| JET ENGINES | Parameter (1) THRUST AUGMENTATION | Parameter (2) OXYGEN FOR PROPELLANTS | Parameter (3) PHYSICAL NATURE OF PROPELLANTS | Parameter (4) SURROUNDING MEDIA | Parameter (5) MOTION OF ENGINE AND WORKING FLUID | Parameter (6) NATURE OF INJECTION OF PROPELLANTS |
|---|---|---|---|---|---|---|
| MORPHOLOGY is concerned with the fundamental pattern of all things. | | | | | | |
| During the War the problem of propulsive power was faced. One promising aspect Seemed to be JET ENGINES. | | | | Air | | |
| The MORPHOLOGICAL approach, when applied to the problem of jet engines produced the six parameters shown on the accompanying MORPHOLOGIZER' slides. | None | Self-contained | Solid | Vacuum | Rotary | Continuous |
| | External | Fuel Plus Free Oxygen From Air | Liquid | Water | Oscillatory | Intermittent |
| When the slides have been set in all possible positions, the Jet Engine problem is before you—for all parameters used. | Internal | Water Reactive Chemical Plus Free Oxygen | Gaseous | Earth | Translatory | |
| | | | | Ice | | |
| 972 types of Jet Engines are indicated. With modifications, an even greater number of jet engines are possible. | | | | Snow | | |

Fig. 5-2

| STRUCTURE OF A DECISION | Parameter (1) PURPOSE OF A HEAT PUMP | Parameter (2) THEORY OF A HEAT PUMP | Parameter (3) TYPES OF BASIC UNITS | Parameter (4) SALES | Parameter (5) INSTALLATION | Parameter (6) DEPENDABILITY | Parameter (7) DEVELOPMENT |
|---|---|---|---|---|---|---|---|
| A company, that had for many years been engaged in the manufacture and distribution of conventional refrigeration-cooling units and combustion heating, has made the general decision to manufacture and distribute some type of HEAT PUMP. | | Employs the Same Basic Principles as an Air-cooled refrigerator | | Customers | | | |
| | | In Summer It Removes Heat From the Building | | Salesman | Space Required | Maintenance | Product |
| | Heating | In Winter It Takes in Heat From Outside Air | Split | Distributors | Structural Modifications | Major Repairs | Market |
| The decision must be made as to the choice of: (1) An Integral Unit. (2) A Split Unit (3) A Split-Integral Unit | Cooling | The Indoor Coil | Integral | Competitors | Noise | Product Failure | Personnel |
| | Ventilating | The Outdoor Coil | Split/Integral | Own Company | Air Ducts | Continuity of Use | Basic Research |
| Approximately one million dollars is involved and, the board of directors must assume the responsibility for making the right decision on a technical matter. | | Refrigerant | | Market | Assembly | Control | Distribution |
| | | Compressor | | Cost | Transportation and Handling | Expected Life | |

Fig. 8-1

| THE STRUCTURE OF CREATIVITY | Parameter (1) THE INTELLECT (J. P. Guilford) | Parameter (2) THE CREATIVE PERSON (A. F. Osborn) | Parameter (3) THE CREATIVE PROCESS (M. S. Allen) | Parameter (4) DETERMINERS OF CREATIVITY (M. S. Allen) | Parameter (5) MORPHOLOGY (F. Zwicky) | Parameter (6) HUMAN NEEDS (A. H. Maslow) | |
|---|---|---|---|---|---|---|---|
| The very complex nature of Creativity, when seen as a way of life, renders its description and illustration a problem of great difficulty. Research in Creative Thinking Decision Making, and Problem solving by the writer since 1939 has produced an overwhelming amount of data, that until recently has defied all efforts to crystallize in any way that would convey to others the concept of creativity that we now hold. The probable fact that the dynamic structure of Creativity shown here will differ from that of every other person is of no real significance. The fact that it may be modified is but one of the values in a *morphological* structure of Creativity. | | Physical Characteristics | Beginning of the Creative Process | Opportunities to Make Discoveries | A Philosophy of Life | | |
| | Sensitivity | Mental Characteristics | Preparation for Creative Activity | Opportunities for Communication | Elimination of Prejudice | Physiological Needs | |
| | Flexibility | Static Personality Characteristics | Synthesis of All Available Knowledge | Aspects of the Personality | A System of Thinking | Safety Needs | |
| | Fluency | Dynamic Personality Characteristics | Orientation to Emerging Goal | Psychological Stimulators | Problem Solving | Belongingness, Love Needs | |
| | Originality | Philosophical Characteristics | Analysis of Problem Now Seen | Psychological Blocks | Evaluation | Esteem Needs | |
| | Memory | Psychological Characteristics | Incubation | Emotional Determiners | Human Relationships | Need for Self Actualization | |
| | | Social Characteristics | The End of the Creative Process | Cultural Determiners | Development of Personality | Need to be Creative | |

| MORPHOLOGY | Parameter (1) PHILOSOPHY | Parameter (2) ELIMINATION OF PREJUDICE | Parameter (3) A SYSTEM OF THINKING | Parameter (4) PROBLEM SOLVING | Parameter (5) EVALUATION | Parameter (6) HUMAN RELATIONSHIPS | Parameter (7) DEVELOPMENT OF THE PERSONALITY |
|---|---|---|---|---|---|---|---|
| The Structure of MORPHOLOGY, as here presented, is an analysis of one of the parameters of the STRUCTURE OF CREATIVITY, by M. S. Allen, visiting Research Associate, Department of Psychology, and instructor of Applied Creativity courses at the University of Southern California. Grateful acknowledgement is made to Dr. F. Zwicky, professor of astrophysics at the California Institute of Technology—for the basic principles of Morphology, which he generously made available to me, through personal conference, reports, letters, and his book *Morphological Astronomy*. | A Systematic Approach to Problems in All Fields | Suspension of Judgement | Creative Thinking Is Imaginative, Healthy, Thinking | Self-Confidence | Avoidance of Premature Evaluation | Consideration of the Same Problem by All Parties | Realization of Potential Genius in All Men |
| | Need for Every Person to Achieve His Creative Potential | Lessening of Usual Resistances to New Ideas | Synthesis | Decision Making | Utilization of Both Conscious & Subconscious experience | Utilization of Multiple View-Points | Stimulus to the Creation of a Richer Life |
| | Basic Pattern of Relationships Between All Things | Prejudice as the Great Block to Creativity | Utilization of the Subconscious | Determination of the Real Problem | Determination of the "King" Value | Open Channels of Communication | Needs and Develops Imagination |
| | Exploration of All Implications Without Prejudice | Reducing Danger of Bit Thinking | Produces Intuition | Multiple Solutions of Complex Problems | Defence Against Individual or Group Pressure | Sense of Freedom While Part of a Rigid Organization | Reduction of Mental Stress |
| | Application of Principles Without Limitations | The Deflation of False Values | Analysis | Flexibility of Total Solution | Evaluation of Partial Solution in Terms of Total Solution | Effects of Mutual Influences | Stimulates Creativity |
| | The Flexibility of Communicable Truth | Foresight | Produces Inventions in a Systematic Manner | Basic Steps of Morphological Problem-Solving | Topological Performance Charts | Industrial Relations | Individual and Group Courage and Certainty |
| | | | | The Morphologizer | | | Recognizes the Reverse Effects of One's Actions |

# INDEX